OBAMA'S LEGACY

DIVERSIONBOOKS

Diversion Books
A Division of Diversion Publishing Corp.
443 Park Avenue South, Suite 1008
New York, New York 10016
www.DiversionBooks.com

For more information, email info@diversionbooks.com

First Diversion Books edition December 2016.
Print ISBN: 978-1-63576-058-3
eBook ISBN: 978-1-63576-057-6

CONTENTS

INTRODUCTION   5

CHAPTER 1: OBAMA'S LEGACY   7
From the Affordable Care Act to the opening of relations
with Cuba, Obama will leave behind a legacy of liberal
achievement   9

CHAPTER 2: THE FIRST BLACK PRESIDENT   19
Some initially heralded his victory as the arrival of a
"post-racial" America   21
In 2015, President Obama and others marked the 50th
anniversary of "Bloody Sunday" in Selma, Ala.   26
A sign of both the digital age and his blackness, Obama has
remixed the image of the American presidency   31
Celebrated by some for racial progress, Obama's presidency
has also drawn racial backlash. Many supporters think he's
faced an unprecedented level of ridicule.   38
In a 2013 trip to Africa, leaders and residents feted Obama
as a native son and a symbol of hope   43
Obama's crusade against a criminal justice system devoid of
'second chances'   49

CHAPTER 3: COMMANDER IN CHIEF   55
Obama as commander in chief: Two experts offer
opposing views   57
For one Washington Post staff writer — a Marine infantry-
man at the time — the surge in Afghanistan was personal   66
A wartime president struggles with the hard questions   70
From Syria to San Bernardino, the rise of the Islamic State
remakes the terrorism equation   76

With his reliance on drones, Obama embraced a deadly,
   high-altitude, secretive war   82

CHAPTER 4: OBAMA'S AMERICA   85
Obama rescued the economy. Could he have done more?   87
Obama's legislative legacy comes down to this question:
   What if?   93
After Obama's reelection, the environment became a
   top priority   103
Guns, grief and gridlock: Time and time again, President
   Obama addressed a nation in mourning   107

CHAPTER 5: OBAMA AND THE WORLD   119
Obama's foreign policy of restraint was both pragmatic and
   problematic   121
Although much of the world still views Obama favorably, the
   dominant emotion in the Middle East is disappointment   128
A renewed relationship with Cuba was one of the administra-
   tion's signature achievements   136
Despite hopes of a strong partnership between the U.S. and
   China, a rocky relationship persisted   142
President Obama put his frequent-flier miles where his
   mouth was: Asia   148
Obama's presidency brought a dramatic upward shift in
   America's reputation around the world   153

CHAPTER 6: THE FIRST FAMILY   157
'The Obamas came from a place we all came from'   159
How Michelle Obama became a singular American voice   169
How the Obamas leveraged fame to advance a political
   agenda   185
For the Obamas, looking cool is part of the job   192
Michelle Obama on White House parenting: 'What on Earth
   am I doing to these babies?'   199
The Obama-Biden bond is among the strongest in White
   House history   205
Seeking a presidential 'pawtograph': Letters from America's
   kids to the first dogs, Sunny and Bo   210

CREDITS   215

INTRODUCTION

Talk of Barack Obama's legacy began much earlier than his final months in office and has intensified as he rounds the final corner of his improbable political career.

Even as some of the political rhetoric longs for a past America, the odds are greater that as the century progresses, Obama will be seen as the pioneer who broke an archaic and distant 220-year period of white male dominance. It was a prejudice-shattering event when he was elected in 2008, and its magnitude is not likely to diminish.

In five parts — The First Black President, Commander in Chief, Obama's America, Obama and the World and The First Family — we explore the triumphs and travails of his historic tenure."

CHAPTER 1

OBAMA'S LEGACY

From the Affordable Care Act to the opening of relations with Cuba, Obama will leave behind a legacy of liberal achievement

By David Maraniss

When Barack Obama worked as a community organizer amid the bleak industrial decay of Chicago's far South Side during the 1980s, he tried to follow a mantra of that profession: Dream of the world as you wish it to be, but deal with the world as it is.

The notion of an Obama presidency was beyond imagining in the world as it was then. But, three decades later, it has happened, and a variation of that saying seems appropriate to the moment: Stop comparing Obama with the president you thought he might be, and deal with the one he has been.

Seven-plus years into his White House tenure, Obama is working through the final months before his presidency slips from present to past, from daily headlines to history books. That will happen at noontime on the 20th of January next year, but the talk of his legacy began much earlier and has intensified as he rounds the final corner of his improbable political career.

Of the many ways of looking at Obama's presidency, the first is to place it in the continuum of his life. The past is prologue for all presidents to one degree or another, even as the job tests them in ways that nothing before could. For Obama, the line connecting his life's story with the reality of what he has been as the 44th president is consistently evident.

The first connection involves Obama's particular form of ambition. His political design arrived relatively late. He was no

President Obama makes a campaign stop during a three-day bus tour in Boone, Iowa, in August 2012. (Nikki Kahn/The Washington Post)

grade school or high school or college leader. Unlike Bill Clinton, he did not have a mother telling everyone that her first-grader would grow up to be president. When Obama was a toddler in Honolulu, his white grandfather boasted that his grandson was a Hawaiian prince, but that was more to explain his skin color than to promote family aspirations.

But once ambition took hold of Obama, it was with an intense sense of mission, sometimes tempered by self-doubt but more often self-assured and sometimes bordering messianic. At the end of his sophomore year at Occidental College, he started to talk about wanting to change the world. At the end of his time as a community organizer in Chicago, he started to talk about how the only way to change the world was through electoral power. When he was defeated for the one and only time in his career in a race for Congress in 2000, he questioned whether he indeed had been chosen for greatness, as he had thought he was, but soon concluded that he needed another test and began preparing to run for the Senate seat from Illinois that he won in 2004.

That is the sensibility he took into the White House. It was not a careless slip when he said during the 2008 campaign that he wanted to emulate Ronald Reagan and change "the trajectory of America" in ways that recent presidents, including Clinton, had been unable to do. Obama did not just want to be president. His mission was to leave a legacy as a president of consequence, the liberal counter to Reagan. To gauge himself against the highest-ranked presidents, and to learn from their legacies, Obama held private White House sessions with an elite group of American historians.

It is now becoming increasingly possible to argue that he has neared his goal. His decisions were ineffective in stemming the human wave of disaster in Syria, and he has thus far failed to close the detention camp at Guantanamo Bay, Cuba, and to make anything more than marginal changes on two domestic issues of importance to him, immigration and gun control. But from the Affordable Care Act to the legalization of same-sex marriage and the nuclear deal with Iran, from the stimulus package that started the slow recovery from the 2008 recession to the Detroit auto industry bailout, from global warming and renewable energy initiatives to the veto of the Keystone pipeline, from the withdrawal of combat troops from Iraq and Afghanistan and the killing of Osama bin Laden to the opening of relations with Cuba, the liberal achievements have added up, however one judges the policies.

This was done at the same time that he faced criticism from various quarters for seeming aloof, if not arrogant, for not being more effective in his dealings with members of Congress of either party, for not being angry enough when some thought he should be, or for not being an alpha male leader.

A PROMISE OF UNITY

His accomplishments were bracketed by two acts of negation by opponents seeking to minimize his authority: first a vow by Republican leaders to do what it took to render him a one-term president; and then, with 11 months left in his second term, a pledge to deny him the appointment of a nominee for the crucial

Supreme Court seat vacated by the death of Antonin Scalia, a conservative icon. Obama's White House years also saw an effort to delegitimize him personally by shrouding his story in fallacious myth — questioning whether he was a foreigner in our midst, secretly born in Kenya, despite records to the contrary, and insinuating that he was a closet Muslim, again defying established fact. Add to that a raucous new techno-political world of unending instant judgments and a decades-long erosion of economic stability for the working class and middle class that was making an increasingly large segment of the population, of various ideologies, feel left behind, uncertain, angry and divided, and the totality was a national condition that was anything but conducive to the promise of unity that brought Obama into the White House.

To the extent that his campaign rhetoric raised expectations that he could bridge the nation's growing political divide, Obama owns responsibility for the way his presidency was perceived. His political rise, starting in 2004, when his keynote convention speech propelled him into the national consciousness, was based on his singular ability to tie his personal story as the son of a father from Kenya and mother from small-town Kansas to some transcendent common national purpose. Unity out of diversity, the ideal of the American mosaic that was constantly being tested, generation after generation, part reality, part myth. Even though Obama romanticized his parents' relationship, which was brief and dysfunctional, his story of commonality was more than a campaign construct; it was deeply rooted in his sense of self.

As a young man, Obama at times felt apart from his high school and college friends of various races and perspectives as he watched them settle into defined niches in culture, outlook and occupation. He told one friend that he felt "large dollops of envy for them" but believed that because of his own life's story, his mixed-race heritage, his experiences in multicultural Hawaii and exotic Indonesia, his childhood without "a structure or tradition to support me," he had no choice but to seek the largest possible embrace of the world. "The only way to assuage my feelings

LEFT: Obama meets with former presidents Bill Clinton and George W. Bush in January 2010 to discuss the recovery and rebuilding efforts in Haiti after a devastating earthquake. (Marvin Joseph/The Washington Post)
RIGHT: A young Obama with his mother, Ann Dunham, in the 1960s. (Family photo via Associated Press)

of isolation are to absorb all the traditions [and all the] classes, make them mine, me theirs," he wrote. He carried that notion with him through his political career in Illinois and all the way to the White House, where it was challenged in ways he had never confronted before.

With most politicians, their strengths are their weaknesses, and their weaknesses are their strengths.

With Obama, one way that was apparent was in his coolness. At various times in his presidency, there were calls from all sides for him to be hotter. He was criticized by liberals for not expressing more anger at Republicans who were stifling his agenda, or at Wall Street financiers and mortgage lenders whose wheeler-dealing helped drag the country into recession. He was criticized by conservatives for not being more vociferous in denouncing Islamic terrorists, or belligerent in standing up to Russian President Vladimir Putin.

His coolness as president can best be understood by the sociological forces that shaped him before he reached the White House. There is a saying among native Hawaiians that goes: Cool head, main thing. This was the culture in which Obama reached adolescence on the island of Oahu, and before that during the four years he lived with his mother in Jakarta. Never show too much. Never rush into things. Maintain a personal reserve and live by your own sense of time. This sensibility was heightened when he developed an affection for jazz, the coolest mode of music, as part of his self-tutorial on black society that he undertook while living with white grandparents in a place where there were very few African Americans. As he entered the political world, the predominantly white society made it clear to him the dangers of coming across as an angry black man. As a community organizer, he refined the skill of leading without being overt about it, making the dispossessed citizens he was organizing feel their own sense of empowerment. As a constitutional law professor at the University of Chicago, he developed an affinity for rational thought.

DIFFERING APPROACHES

All of this created a president who was comfortable coolly working in his own way at his own speed, waiting for events to turn his way.

Was he too cool in his dealings with other politicians? One way to consider that question is by comparing him with Clinton. Both came out of geographic isolation, Hawaii and southwest Arkansas, far from the center of power, in states that had never before offered up presidents. Both came out of troubled families defined by fatherlessness and alcoholism. Both at various times felt a sense of abandonment. Obama had the additional quandary of trying to figure out his racial identity. And the two dealt with their largely similar situations in diametrically different ways.

Rather than deal with the problems and contradictions of his life head-on, Clinton became skilled at moving around and past them. He had an insatiable need to be around people for affirmation. As a teenager, he would ask a friend to come over to the house just to watch him do a crossword puzzle. His life became all about survival and reading the room. He kept shoeboxes full of file cards of the names and phone numbers of people who might help him someday. His nature was to always move forward. He would wake up each day and forgive himself and keep going. His motto became "What's next?" He refined these skills to become a political force of nature, a master of transactional politics. This got him to the White House, and into trouble in the White House, and out of trouble again, in acycle of loss and recovery.

Obama spent much of his young adulthood, from when he left Hawaii for the mainland and college in 1979 to the time he left Chicago for Harvard Law School nearly a decade later, trying to figure himself out, examining the racial, cultural, personal, sociological and political contradictions that life threw at him. He internalized everything, first withdrawing from the world during a period in New York City and then slowly reentering it as he was finding his identity as a community organizer in Chicago.

Rather than plow forward relentlessly, like Clinton, Obama slowed down. He woke up each day and wrote in his journal, analyzing the world and his place in it. He emerged from that process with a sense of self that helped him rise in politics all the way to the White House, then led him into difficulties in the White House, or at least criticism for the way he operated. His sensibility was that if he could resolve the contradictions of his own life, why couldn't the rest of the country resolve the larger contradictions of American life? Why couldn't Congress? The answer from Republicans was that his actions were different from his words, and that while he talked the language of compromise, he did not often act on it. He had built an impressive organization to get elected, but it relied more on the idea of Obama than on a long history of personal contacts. He did not have a figurative equivalent of Clinton's shoebox full of allies, and he did not share his Democratic predecessor's profound need to be around people. He was not as interested in the personal side of politics that was so second nature to presidents such as Clinton and Lyndon Johnson.

Politicians of both parties complained that Obama seemed distant. He was not calling them often enough. When he could be schmoozing with members of Congress, cajoling them and making them feel important, he was often back in the residence having dinner with his wife, Michelle, and their two daughters, or out golfing with the same tight group of high school chums and White House subordinates.

Here again, some history provided context. Much of Obama's early life had been a long search for home, which he finally found with Michelle and their girls, Malia and Sasha. There were times when Obama was an Illinois state senator and living for a few months at a time in a hotel room in Springfield, when Michelle made clear her unhappiness with his political obsession, and the sense of home that he had strived so hard to find was jeopardized. Once he reached the White House, with all the demands on his time, if there was a choice, he was more inclined to be with his family than hang out with politicians. A weakness in one sense, a strength in another, enriching the image of the first-ever black first family.

A COMPLEX QUESTION

The fact that Obama was the first black president, and that his family was the first African American first family, provides him with an uncontested hold on history. Not long into his presidency, even to mention that seemed beside the point, if not tedious, but it was a prejudice-shattering event when he was elected in 2008, and its magnitude is not likely to diminish. Even as some of the political rhetoric this year longs for a past America, the odds are greater that as the century progresses, no matter what happens in the 2016 election, Obama will be seen as the pioneer who broke an archaic and distant 220-year period of white male dominance.

But what kind of black president has he been?

Obama is sworn in as the 44th president by Chief Justice John G. Roberts Jr. on Jan. 20, 2009. (Jonathan Newton/The Washington Post)

His life illuminates the complexity of that question. His white mother, who conscientiously taught him black history at an early age but died nearly a decade before her son reached the White House, would have been proud that he broke the racial barrier. But she also inculcated him in the humanist idea of the universality of humankind, a philosophy that her life exemplified as she married a Kenyan and later an Indonesian and worked to help empower women in many of the poorest countries in the world. Obama eventually found his own comfort as a black man with a black family, but his public persona, and his political persona, was more like his mother's.

At various times during his career, Obama faced criticism from some African Americans that, because Obama did not grow up in a minority community and received an Ivy League education, he was not "black enough." That argument was one of the reasons he lost that 2000 congressional race to Bobby L. Rush, a former Black Panther, but fortunes shift and attitudes along with them; there was no more poignant and revealing scene at Obama's final State of the Union address to Congress than Rep. Rush waiting anxiously at the edge of the aisle and reaching out in the hope of recognition from the passing president.

As president, Obama rarely broke character to show what was inside. He was reluctant to bring race into the political discussion, and never publicly stated what many of his supporters believed: that some of the antagonism toward his presidency was rooted in racism. He wished to be judged by the content of his presidency rather than the color of his skin. One exception came after February 2012, when Trayvon Martin, an unarmed black teenager, was shot and killed in Florida by a gun-toting neighborhood zealot. In July 2013, commenting on the verdict in the case, Obama talked about the common experience of African American men being followed when shopping in a department store, or being passed up by a taxi on the street, or a car door lock clicking as they walked by — all of which he said had happened to him. He said Trayvon Martin could have been his son, and then added, "another way of saying that is: Trayvon Martin could have been me 35 years ago."

Nearly two years later, in June 2015, Obama hit what might be considered the most powerful emotional note of his presidency, a legacy moment, by finding a universal message in black spiritual expression. Time after time during his two terms, he had performed the difficult task of trying to console the country after another mass shooting, choking up with tears whenever he talked about little children being the victims, as they had been in 2012 at Sandy Hook Elementary School in Newtown, Conn. Now he was delivering the heart-rending message one more time, nearing the end of a eulogy in Charleston, S.C., for the Rev. Clementa Pinckney, one of nine African Americans killed by a young white gunman during a prayer service at Emanuel African Methodist Episcopal Church. It is unlikely that any other president could have done what Barack Obama did that day, when all the separate parts of his life story came together with a national longing for reconciliation as he started to sing, "Amazing grace, how sweet the sound, that saved a wretch like me. . . ."

CHAPTER 2

THE FIRST
BLACK PRESIDENT

Some initially heralded his victory as the arrival of a "post-racial" America

By Peniel Joseph

Barack Obama's watershed 2008 election and the presidency that followed profoundly altered the aesthetics of American democracy, transforming the Founding Fathers' narrow vision of politics and citizenship into something more expansive and more elegant. The American presidency suddenly looked very different, and for a moment America felt different, too.

The Obama victory helped fulfill one of the great ambitions of the civil rights struggle by showcasing the ability of extraordinarily talented black Americans to lead and excel in all facets of American life. First lady Michelle Obama, and daughters Sasha and Malia, extended this reimagining of black American life by providing a conspicuous vision of a healthy, loving and thriving African American family that defies still-prevalent racist stereotypes.

But some interpreted Obama's triumph as much more.

The victory was heralded as the arrival of a "post-racial" America, one in which the nation's original sin of racial slavery and post-Reconstruction Jim Crow discrimination had finally been absolved by the election of a black man as commander in chief. For a while, the nation basked in a racially harmonious afterglow.

A black president would influence generations of young children to embrace a new vision of American citizenship. The "Obama Coalition" of African American, white, Latino, Asian American and Native American voters had helped usher in an era

Members of the crowd in Gary, Ind., seek to shake the candidate's hand or touch his head as he thanks them for their support in October 2008. (Linda Davidson/The Washington Post)

in which institutional racism and pervasive inequality would fade as Americans embraced the nation's multicultural promise.

Seven years later, such profound optimism seems misplaced. Almost immediately, the Obama presidency unleashed racial furies that have only multiplied over time. From the tea party's racially tinged attacks on the president's policy agenda to the "birther" movement's more overtly racist fantasies asserting that Obama was not even an American citizen, the national racial climate grew more, and not less, fraught.

If racial conflict, in the form of birthers, tea partiers and gnawing resentments, implicitly shadowed Obama's first term, it erupted into open warfare during much of his second. The Supreme Court's 2013 decision in the *Shelby v. Holder* case gutted Voting Rights Act enforcement, throwing into question the signal achievement of the civil rights movement's heroic period.

Beginning with the 2012 shooting death of black teenager Trayvon Martin in Florida, the nation reopened an intense debate on the continued horror of institutional racism evidenced by a string of high-profile deaths of black men, women, boys and girls at the hands of law enforcement.

The organized demonstrations, protests and outrage of a new generation of civil rights activists turned the hashtag #BlackLivesMatter into the clarion call for a new social justice movement. Black Lives Matter activists have forcefully argued that the U.S. criminal justice system represents a gateway to racial oppression, one marked by a drug war that disproportionately targets, punishes and warehouses young men and women of color. In her bestselling book "The New Jim Crow," legal scholar Michelle Alexander argued that mass incarceration represents a racial caste system that echoes the pervasive, structural inequality of a system of racial apartheid that persists.

Obama's first-term caution on race matters was punctured by his controversial remarks that police "acted stupidly" in the mistaken identity arrest of Henry Louis Gates Jr., Harvard University's prominent African American studies professor, in 2009. Four years later he entered the breach once more by proclaiming that if he had a son, "he'd look like Trayvon."

In the aftermath of racial unrest in Ferguson, Mo., and Baltimore, and a racially motivated massacre in Charleston, S.C., Obama went further. In 2015, Obama found his voice in a series of stirring speeches in Selma, Ala., and Charleston, where he acknowledged America's long and continuous history of racial injustice.

Policy-wise Obama has launched a private philanthropic effort, My Brother's Keeper, designed to assist low-income black boys, and became the first president to visit a federal prison in a call for prison reform that foreshadowed the administration's efforts to release federal inmates facing long sentences on relatively minor drug charges.

Despite these efforts, many of Obama's African American supporters have expressed profound disappointment over the president's refusal to forcefully pursue racial and economic justice policies for his most loyal political constituency.

From this perspective, the Obama presidency has played out as a cruel joke on members of the African American community who, despite providing indispensable votes, critical support and unstinting loyalty, find themselves largely shut out from the nation's post-Great Recession economic recovery. Blacks have, critics suggested, traded away substantive policy demands for the largely symbolic psychological and emotional victory of having a black president and first family in the White House for eight years.

Others find that assessment harsh, noting that Obama's most impressive policy achievements have received scant promotion from the White House or acknowledgment in the mainstream media.

History will decide the full measure of the importance, success, failures and shortcomings of the Obama presidency. With regard to race, Obama's historical significance is ensured; only his impact and legacy are up for debate. In retrospect, the burden of transforming America's tortured racial history in two four-year presidential terms proved impossible, even as its promise helped to catapult Obama to the nation's highest office.

Obama's presidency elides important aspects of the civil rights struggle, especially the teachings of the Rev. Martin Luther King Jr. King, for a time, served as the racial justice consciousness for two presidents — John F. Kennedy and Lyndon B. Johnson. Many who hoped Obama might be able to serve both roles — as president and racial justice advocate — have been disappointed. Yet there is a revelatory clarity in that disappointment, proving that Obama is not King or Frederick Douglass, but Abraham Lincoln, Kennedy and Johnson. Even a black president, perhaps especially a black president, could not untangle racism's Gordian knot on the body politic. Yet in acknowledging the limitations of Obama's presidency on healing racial divisions and the shortcomings of his policies in uplifting black America, we may reach a newfound political maturity that recognizes that no one person — no matter how powerful — can single-handedly rectify structures of inequality constructed over centuries.

Peniel Joseph is professor of history and director of the Center for the Study of Race and Democracy and the LBJ School of Public Affairs at the University of Texas.

In 2015, President Obama and others marked the 50th anniversary of "Bloody Sunday" in Selma, Ala.

By Terence Samuel

In the spring of 1965, Selma, Ala., inscribed itself on the American consciousness as a place of struggle and courage, a bloody battlefield in the war on racial injustice. The march from Selma to Montgomery was a culmination of long-running voting-rights protests outside of the Dallas County Courthouse in Selma, launched by Martin Luther King Jr. in January 1965. On the morning of March 7, 1965, about 500 protesters left Brown Chapel AME Church for the Edmund Pettus Bridge and Highway 80, headed for Montgomery. At the other end of the bridge, rows and rows of Alabama state troopers waited with billy clubs and tear gas. State trooper Maj. John Cloud used his bullhorn to declare the march an "unlawful assembly" and told the marchers they had two minutes to disperse. They didn't. Instead, they went to their knees and prayed. Before long, the troopers pounced. The television images of the attack dramatically changed public opinion and led to passage of the Voting Rights Act.

Fifty years later, President Obama arrived in the central Alabama city to honor and remember the early civil-rights warriors, some of whom were violently assaulted by baton-wielding police officers as they tried to secure the right to vote for black people all over the South. Despite the dark associations of violence, Obama said that Selma should be a place of optimism: "Selma teaches us, too, that action requires that we shed our cynicism. For when it

President Obama crosses the Edmund Pettus Bridge while holding hands with Rep. John Lewis (D-Ga.), left, and Amelia Boynton Robinson, both of whom were beaten by state troopers during the Bloody Sunday march in 1965. Boynton was one of the organizers of that march. She died at 104, six months after this photo was taken. (Jacquelyn Martin/Associated Press)

Alabama state troopers swing nightsticks to break up the march in Selma, Ala., on March 7, 1965. (Associated Press)

Tear gas fills the air as state troopers break up the march on the Edmund Pettus Bridge on March 7, 1965. (Associated Press)

We are the people Em... ...ote of, "who for truth and honor's sa...
who are "never too tired, so long as we can see far enough."

That's what America is. Not stock photos or feeble attempts to define some as more American
as others. We respect the past, but we don't pine for it. We don't fear the future; we grab for i
America is not some fragile thing; we are large, in the words of Whitman, containing multitud
We are boisterous and full of energy, perpetually young in spirit. That's why someone like Jo
Lewis at the ripe age of 25 could lead a mighty march.

CLOCKWISE FROM ABOVE:

A piece of a copy of the speech that President Obama delivered at the foot of the Edmund Pettus Bridge on March 7, 2015. (Marvin Joseph/The Washington Post)

A man sits near the Selma voting-rights mural on March 3, 2015. (Jahi Chikwendiu/The Washington Post)

Civil-rights marchers again set out to march from Selma to Montgomery on March 21, 1965. The 50-mile march prompted Congress to pass the Voting Rights Act. (Associated Press).

President Obama hugs Rep. John Lewis (D-Ga.) during the event marking the 50th anniversary of Bloody Sunday. (Saul Loeb/Agence France-Presse via Getty Images).

comes to the pursuit of justice, we can afford neither complacency nor despair."

For Obama, Selma was a clarifying moment: In his mind, what happened in Selma in 1965, and in America over the next 50 years, was exactly what America was about.

"There are places and moments in America where this nation's destiny has been decided. Many are sites of war — Concord and Lexington, Appomattox, Gettysburg. Others are sites that symbolize the daring of America's character — Independence Hall and Seneca Falls, Kitty Hawk and Cape Canaveral. Selma is such a place," Obama said, standing on the Edmund Pettus Bridge. "In one afternoon 50 years ago, so much of our turbulent history — the stain of slavery and anguish of civil war, the yoke of segregation and tyranny of Jim Crow, the death of four little girls in Birmingham, and the dream of a Baptist preacher — all that history met on this bridge."

Obama had decided that he would use the 50th anniversary of what became known as Bloody Sunday to talk about the America in which he believed. He invoked Jackie Robinson and Langston Hughes, Walt Whitman and Ralph Waldo Emerson.

"What could more profoundly vindicate the idea of America than plain and humble people — unsung, the downtrodden, the dreamers not of high station, not born to wealth or privilege, not of one religious tradition but many — coming together to shape their country's course?"

Obama used the Selma anniversary to lay out a crystallized idea of why he thinks America is exceptional, and it had less to do with power than with imperfection: "What greater expression of faith in the American experiment than this, what greater form of patriotism is there than the belief that America is not yet finished, that we are strong enough to be self-critical, that each successive generation can look upon our imperfections and decide that it is in our power to remake this nation to more closely align with our highest ideals?"

A sign of both the digital age and his blackness, Obama has remixed the image of the American presidency

By Terence Samuel

Barack Obama's candidacy and subsequent presidency changed forever the way we see the American presidency. Obviously, he looked different from the men who preceded him, but he also brought a different sensibility and aesthetic to the office. Some of the change was traceable to the time he rose to power, which explains the selfies and tweets, and the hip-hop references. Others felt singular to his role as the first black president. The result, in both cases, was a series of striking and novel presidential images and moments.

With Obama's ascent, the presidency began to look completely different from anything in memory. In this April 2008 photo taken at a town hall meeting in Raleigh, N.C., during his campaign, a confident Obama brushes some imaginary dirt off his shoulder, miming a popular hip-hop anthem and using it as a metaphor for how he deals with detractors and critics. Some of those critics would later see this kind of confidence as arrogance.

Among the many novel fascinations about the nation's first black president was his hair: its change in color over time, its length. In September 2014, the president visited Clarence Tinker Elementary School at MacDill Air Force Base in Tampa, where he and first-grader Edwin Caleb traded hair pats. After Edwin said he had short hair, Obama touched the boy's head and said: "Mine, too. Here, want to touch it?"

On the night in June 2008 when he secured enough delegates

Young, cool and black: Barack Obama at a town hall meeting in Raleigh, N.C., during his campaign. (Jae C. Hong/Associated Press)

In the Oval Office in 2009, President Obama bends down to allow Jacob Philadelphia to feel his hair. (Pete Souza/The White House).

State of the head: First-grader Edwin Caleb touches the president's hair during Obama's visit to Clarence Tinker Elementary School in September 2014. (Lawrence Jackson/The White House).

First fist bumps: The first recorded instance of a celebratory "dap" in American political history. (Scott Olson/Getty Images)

The first night: The first couple takes the floor for the first dance at the Neighborhood Ball on Inauguration Day in 2009. (Richard A. Lipski/ The Washington Post)

to win the Democratic nomination for president, Obama addressed a crowd at the Xcel Energy Center in St. Paul, Minn. Before the speech, he and his wife celebrated with what The Washington Post described as "the fist bump heard 'round the world." The gesture felt so overwhelmingly black and so new in national politics that it spawned a huge debate about cultural significance. "He wears his cultural blackness all over the place," observed writer Ta-Nehisi Coates. Obama explained it differently: "It captured what I love about my wife. There's an irreverence about her and sense that for all the hoopla, that I'm her husband and sometimes we'll do silly things, and yet she's proud of me and she gives me some credit once in a while that I actually pull some things off."

It is hard to overstate the level of excitement that gripped Washington during Obama's first inauguration. More than 2 million people crammed onto the Mall for his swearing-in and to hear the new president say: "On this day, we gather because we have chosen hope over fear, unity of purpose over conflict and discord. On this day, we come to proclaim an end to the petty grievances

POTUS sings the blues: Obama and B.B. King at a blues all-stars gathering in the White House East Room. (Pete Souza/The White House)

and false promises, the recriminations and worn-out dogmas that for far too long have strangled our politics."

President Obama has occasionally deployed his singing voice in public with soulful or spiritual music. First, it was a snippet of Al Green's "Let's Stay Together" at a fundraiser at the Apollo Theatre in New York in January 2012. A month later, when a group of blues all-stars gathered in the East Room of the White House for a "Red, White and Blues" concert, legendary guitarist Buddy Guy goaded Obama into joining in the closing number, "Sweet Home Chicago." Mick Jagger handed the president the microphone, and the commander in chief crooned: "Come on, baby, don't you wanna go." B.B. King joined in — "Same old place" — and the president closed out the number: "Sweet home Chicago." Among some of the participants that evening were, onstage from left: Troy "Trombone Shorty" Andrews, Jeff Beck, Derek Trucks, Gary Clark Jr. and B.B. King.

Among the most enduring critiques of the Obama presidency was an assertion that Obama was too cerebral, too emotionally distant, too aloof. For all the praise for his putative cool, there was an equal measure of criticism that he was sometimes too laid back and not angry enough. That debate produced a lot of commentary

Calm and collected: Obama speaks at the White House Correspondents' Association Dinner in Washington in April 2015 as comedian Keegan-Michael Key plays the role of Luther, Obama's "anger translator." (Yuri Gripas/Agence France-Presse via Getty Images)

A "Soul Plane" moment: Obama talks with aides aboard Marine One on Aug. 9, 2010. (Pete Souza/The White House)

A familiar refrain: Obama sings "Amazing Grace" while eulogizing the Rev. Clementa Pinckney, a South Carolina state senator, on June 26, 2015, in Charleston, S.C. (Win McNamee/Getty Images)

on whether Obama's slowness to anger was related to his blackness, lessons learned in the limits of black rage and whether he was avoiding being cast as the stereotypical angry black man. In a 2012 essay in the Atlantic, Ta-Nehisi Coates framed the problem this way: "Part of Obama's genius is a remarkable ability to soothe race consciousness among whites. Any black person who's worked in the professional world is well acquainted with this trick. But never has it been practiced at such a high level, and never have its limits been so obviously exposed. This need to talk in dulcet tones, to never be angry regardless of the offense, bespeaks a strange and compromised integration indeed." Obama addressed the problem most explicitly in a comedy sketch at the 2015 White House Correspondents' Association Dinner, in which comedian Keegan-Michael Key appeared as Luther, his "anger translator." Obama stuck to his usual "dulcet tones" while Key decoded the hidden anger.

This moment captured by White House photographer Pete Souza is a simple shot of the president and his top aides on Marine One, traveling from the White House to Joint Base Andrews and then on to Texas for the day. The group includes Valerie Jarrett in the far corner, with the president, Bill Burton and Patrick Gaspard all looking at Reggie Love — a small group of five, every one of them black. "We joked that it was 'Soul Plane,'" Burton told New York Magazine. "And we've often joked about it since — that it was the first time in history only black people were on that helicopter."

Obama's June 2015 eulogy for the Rev. Clementa Pinckney in Charleston, S.C., will be remembered for Obama's singing of "Amazing Grace." He was at Emanuel African Methodist Episcopal Church, also known as Mother Emanuel, to honor the nine people killed there by a young white man. But the eulogy also served as a meditation on race during his presidency. Before he broke into song, he said: "None of us can or should expect a transformation in race relations overnight. Every time something like this happens, somebody says we have to have a conversation about race. We talk a lot about race. There's no shortcut. And we don't need more talk." The eulogy sounded so much like a sermon that the minister who closed the service offered his thanks to "the Reverend President."

Celebrated by some for racial progress, Obama's presidency has also drawn racial backlash. Many supporters think he's faced an unprecedented level of ridicule.

By Terence Samuel

Barack Obama's presidency will always be tethered to the history of race in America. It has, so far, been offered as Exhibit A of how far the country has moved toward overcoming its ugly racial past. Others use it, with equal force, to make the opposite point, that race-based antagonism is so endemic to the American way of life that it will take more than the election of a black president to move the country beyond its long traditions of racism and discrimination.

Obama is generally in the first, more optimistic camp. In a 2015 interview for the podcast "WTF With Marc Maron," he said: "I always tell young people, in particular, do not say that nothing has changed when it comes to race in America, unless you've lived through being a black man in the 1950s or '60s or '70s. It is incontrovertible that race relations have improved significantly during my lifetime and yours."

Incontrovertible, indeed.

But from the very beginning, Obama's ascendance produced a huge backlash that was undeniably racist in nature, tied to what he has described euphemistically as his "unique demographic."

In the days before the 2008 election, a life-size likeness of the candidate was found hanging from a tree at the University

A clown wears a mask intended to look like President Obama at the Missouri State Fair in August 2013. (Jameson Hsieh/Associated Press)

of Kentucky in Lexington. In the town of Wolfeboro, N.H., an elected member of the police commission was forced to resign in 2014 after he acknowledged and refused to apologize for publicly referring to Obama as a "nigger" while in a local restaurant. Robert Copeland was head of the town's three-member police commission when a relatively new resident of Wolfeboro heard him use the slur to describe the president. When she learned who Copeland was, she complained to town officials, who confronted the 82-year-old Copeland. He expanded on his feelings about Obama: "I believe I did use the 'N' word in reference to the current occupant of the Whitehouse," Copeland wrote in an email to the other police commissioners. "For this, I do not apologize — he meets and exceeds my criteria for such."

The previous summer, organizers of the Missouri State Fair barred a rodeo clown with an Obama mask after complaints that it was racist. Fair organizers called the clown display "inappropriate and disrespectful."

Rep. Joe Wilson (R-S.C.) shouts out "you lie!" during Obama's address to a Joint Session of Congress concerning health care in September 2009. (Melina Mara/The Washington Post)

Many who support the president, particularly many African Americans who feel a deep racial pride in his achievements, feel that he has been subject to an unprecedented level of ridicule, which they attribute to race. In an interview with the BBC, Oprah Winfrey said: "There is a level of disrespect for the office that occurs. And that occurs, in some cases, and maybe even many cases, because he's African American."

Former president Jimmy Carter told "NBC Nightly News" in 2009: "I think an overwhelming portion of the intensely demonstrated animosity toward President Barack Obama is based on the fact that he is a black man."

Obama has suggested, in his typically oblique way, that race may be driving some of the fierce opposition he has faced. In an interview with NPR, he said: "If you are referring to specific strains in the Republican Party that suggest that somehow I'm different, I'm Muslim, I'm disloyal to the country, etc., which unfortunately is pretty far out there and gets some traction in certain pockets of the Republican Party, and that have been articulated by some of their elected officials, what I'd say there is that that's probably pretty specific to me and who I am and my background, and that in some ways I may represent change that worries them."

The list of affronts famously includes Rep. Joe Wilson (R-S.C.) yelling "you lie!" at the president as Obama addressed a joint session of Congress in 2009; then-Arizona governor Jan Brewer sticking a finger in his face during a heated discussion about immigration on an airport tarmac in Phoenix in 2012; and then-House speaker John A. Boehner's decision in 2015 to invite the Israeli prime minister to address Congress about the dangers of dealing with Iran without informing the White House.

But Obama has been a broadly polarizing figure, and one of the big questions in trying to assess the legacy of his presidency is how to untangle the fierce political and ideological disagreement he evoked from the race-based hostility that his presidency aroused.

Even some of those willing to acknowledge their racial animus toward the president say that the opposition is driven by ideological or political differences, not race.

Noted white nationalist Jared Taylor has explained the backlash against Obama as an overall failure of the integrationist ideal, saying that people of different races were not meant to live together and that many people were simply reverting to the norm by turning against the idea that Obama's election was somehow racially transformative. Taylor's racial prejudices are on open display; he believes America should be a white country and that the Obama presidency is just another milestone in the wrong direction.

But many of the president's supporters see a direct line between those prejudices and the rodeo clown, the n-word references and Wilson's "you lie" moment. "That racism inclination still exists," Carter said. "And I think it's bubbled up to the surface because of the belief among many white people, not just in the South but around the country, that African Americans are not qualified to lead this great country."

In a 2013 trip to Africa, leaders and residents feted Obama as a native son and a symbol of hope

By David Nakamura

Zoom in, and the scene is like so many others: An American family on vacation, touring a historical site abroad. The father is in khakis and a navy windbreaker, the mother in a sweater and sensible pumps, and their two school-age daughters in casual wear and sneakers, arms crossed and looking slightly bored as an elderly tour guide explains the global significance of a pile of limestone rocks.

Pan back now from the tight frame to the rim of the rock quarry that encircles them, the television news cameras perched above, a convoy of black security vehicles, the Secret Service snipers in combat gear and rifles hidden in the brush, a U.S. Marine helicopter bearing the presidential seal. An even wider frame reveals a view of all of Robben Island, off the coast of Cape Town, South Africa, a beautiful but barren speck on the globe, once so loaded with political urgency and, now, nearly three decades later, at the center of attention again.

President Obama and his family have arrived, in the summer of 2013, to tour the place where one of Obama's personal and political heroes, Nelson Mandela, the anti-apartheid revolutionary and former president of South Africa, spent nearly two decades behind bars and was forced to perform hard labor in this very limestone quarry.

It is a visit that so many have waited so long for, the first black leader of the world's most powerful nation paying homage

President Obama peers out of former South African president Nelson Mandela's prison cell on Robben Island. (Carolyn Kaster/ Associated Press)

The note that Obama and the first lady signed in a guest book at Robben Island in June 2013. (Saul Loeb/Agence France-Presse via Getty Images)

Obama looks out from the Door of No Return at the House of Slaves, a memorial to the Atlantic slave trade on Senagal's Goree Island, in June 2013. (Evan Vucci/ Associated Press) to a global icon of black struggle. Together the two men and their presidencies seemed to represent the triumph of two great liberation movements: the American struggle for civil rights and the international fight against South African apartheid.

It was Mandela's struggle and writings that had persuaded a young Obama to take his first steps into political activism during his years at Occidental College and at Harvard Law School in the early 1990s.

In his 1995 book, "Dreams From My Father," Obama wrote that Mandela, from afar, was one of his male role models in the absence of his own father. Mandela was released from prison in 1990. Obama had visited Robben Island once before, in 2006 as a U.S. senator from Illinois, but not as president and not with his family.

And yet for Obama, the return is bittersweet.

A day earlier, 900 miles away in Johannesburg, the president's motorcade had pulled up to the Nelson Mandela Center of Memory, where Obama met privately with Mandela's daughters Makaziwe Mandela and Zindzi Mandela Hlongwane, as well as a number of his grandchildren. Mandela, 94, was in the hospital, severely ill, and Obama had chosen not to visit the ailing icon out of respect for his health concerns.

Obama, then 51, instead spoke by telephone with Mandela's wife, Graça Machel, who was at her husband's side in the hospital.

"I don't need a photo-op, and the last thing I want to do is to be in any way obtrusive," Obama had told reporters on Air Force One during a flight from Senegal to South Africa on a six-day trip to three African nations, his first extended visit to the continent while in office. His final stop would be Tanzania.

"The main message we'll want to deliver, if not directly to him but to his family, is simply our profound gratitude for his leadership all these years," said the president, who had met Mandela just once, in 2005, when Mandela already had become frail.

A single photo exists of their brief, unscheduled meeting at the Four Seasons Hotel in Washington, a snapshot taken by an Obama aide. The senator is cast in silhouette by the window, standing and shaking hands with the seated Mandela, who is more clearly lit, a walking cane within the older man's reach.

If that private meeting was not yet a symbolic passing of the torch — Mandela only vaguely knew who he was meeting — Obama's visits to Johannesburg and Cape Town in 2013 are viewed as one.

Obama and Mandela are "bound by history as the first black presidents of their respective countries," South African President Jacob Zuma said after a meeting with Obama. "Both carry the dreams of millions of people of Africa and the diaspora who were previously oppressed."

Mandela would die six months later.

Throughout his tour, Obama is feted as a native son, even though he has elected not to visit Kenya, his father's homeland. There is a palpable sense that he remains a symbol of hope, despite the fact that Obama's Africa policy on trade, development and health care had been criticized for not being as robust as those of his two predecessors, George W. Bush and Bill Clinton.

"Welcome home, Mr. President," posters in Senegal read. In South Africa, children wore clothing with his likeness. And in Tanzania, the government renamed the boulevard outside the presidential palace "Barack Obama Drive."

In Cape Town, during a discussion on AIDS policy, the Archbishop Desmond Tutu told the U.S. president: "When you became the first black incumbent of the White House, you don't know what you did for our psyches. My wife sat in front of the TV with tears running down her face as she watched the celebration with you in Chicago. You won. And we won."

Onlookers chuckled, but the older man, sitting next to Obama at a long, thin table, leaned in closer. "Your success is our success. Your failure, whether you like it or not, is our failure," he said slowly. "And so we want to assure you that we pray for you to be a great success."

Obama looked uncertain while Tutu talked — here was a man

who, like Mandela, had fought apartheid and inspired a younger Obama. Now, Tutu was handing him their mantle.

And yet, the American leader had another goal for his Africa trip than simply basking in the glory of his own reflection: inspiring the next generation of political leaders.

During a town-hall-style discussion with 650 students at the University of Johannesburg's Soweto campus, and with thousands more watching across the continent on a live broadcast, Obama spoke optimistically of young Africans whose politics and activism would help overcome the historical residue of apartheid and slavery, and the corruption in many modern-day African nations.

The president quoted from Robert Kennedy's address in Cape Town in 1966, saying the challenges of our world demand "the qualities of youth; not a time in life, but a state of mind, a temper of the will, a quality of the imagination, a predominance of courage over timidity, of the appetite for adventure over the love of ease."

So zoom in again on the Obamas in the limestone quarry, where the air is still, the sun is bright and they are listening to Ahmed Mohamed Kathrada, then 83, who spent 18 years here as a political prisoner.

The president, wearing sunglasses, turns toward Malia, then 15, and Sasha, then 12. A television boom microphone captures his words.

"One thing you guys might not be aware of is that the idea of political nonviolence first took root here in South Africa because Mahatma Gandhi was a lawyer here in South Africa. Here is where he did his first political activism. When he went back to India, the principles ultimately led to Indian independence, and what Gandhi did inspired Martin Luther King."

Mandela, Gandhi, King. The names of men who changed the world ring out in the stillness of the barren island where Obama has come to pay his respects.

Obama's crusade against a criminal justice system devoid of 'second chances'

By Sari Horwitz and Wesley Lowery

Criminal justice was always a priority issue for Barack Obama. "Since my first campaign, I've talked about how, in too many cases, our criminal justice system ends up being a pipeline from under-funded, inadequate schools to overcrowded jails," he declared in the summer of 2015.

But over the course of his presidency, he became something of a crusader, prodded in part by a growing national movement dedicated to unmasking the discrimination and injustice that so often color and guide the interactions between law enforcement officials and people of color.

Over time, Obama became an increasingly forceful voice, pledging to address the epidemic of incarceration that dispropor-tionately affects people of color, and speaking out against what he described as "a long history of inequity in the criminal justice system in America."

In July 2015, six-and a half years into his presidency, Obama gave his first major criminal justice speech to a crowd of more than 3,000 at the NAACP convention in Philadelphia. He declared that the U.S. criminal justice system was not as "smart" as it needs to be: "It's not keeping us as safe as it should be. It is not as fair as it should be. Mass incarceration makes our country worse off, and we need to do something about it."

But Obama was speaking at a time of crisis. In the previous year a new activism had taken hold across the country after several

President Obama, with Charles Samuels, right, then-director of the Bureau of Prisons, and Ronald Warlick, a correctional officer, tours a cell block at the El Reno Federal Correctional Institution in El Reno, Okla., in July 2015. (Saul Loeb/Agence France-Presse via Getty Images)

unarmed black men and boys died in confrontations with police officers, many of them recorded with cell phone video and police body cameras. They seemed ubiquitous on the internet, and the president saw it as a moment of reckoning.

"In recent years the eyes of more Americans have been opened to this truth," Obama said. "Partly because of cameras, partly because of tragedy, partly because the statistics cannot be ignored, we can't close our eyes anymore."

The next day, Obama became the first sitting president to visit a federal prison when he went to the El Reno Federal Correctional Institution in Oklahoma. His purpose was clear: "I'm going to shine a spotlight on this issue, because while the people in our prisons have made some mistakes — and sometimes big mistakes — they are also Americans, and we have to make sure that as they do their time and pay back their debt to society that we are increasing the possibility that they can turn their lives around."

The images of the president of the United States inside a federal lockup were striking enough: His suggestion that he could have ended up there as a prisoner was startling.

"When they describe their youth, these are young people who made mistakes that aren't that different from the mistakes I made, and the mistakes that a lot of you guys made," Obama said. "The difference is that they did not have the kind of support structures, the second chances, the resources that would allow them to survive those mistakes."

Obama and former U.S. attorney general Eric H. Holder Jr. helped launch a national conversation about mass incarceration and put in place several new criminal justice reform measures.

As part of a 2013 plan called Smart on Crime, Holder directed his prosecutors nationwide to stop bringing charges that would impose harsh mandatory minimum sentences, except in the most egregious cases.

Holder said that criminal justice reform is a deeply personal issue for the president. He and Obama have had countless conversations over the years — since they met in 2004 — about how this country prosecutes and incarcerates its citizens, especially men and women of color.

Obama's speech to the NAACP came three and a half years after Trayvon Martin, 17, was killed by George Zimmerman in Florida; a year after Eric Garner, 43, died after a police officer put him in a chokehold on Staten Island; 11 months after Michael Brown, 18, was shot and killed in Ferguson, Mo., by Officer Darren Wilson; eight months after Tamir Rice, 12, was killed by a Cleveland police officer; and three months before Walter Scott in South Carolina and Freddie Gray in Baltimore died after encounters with police officers.

The Michel Brown killing seemed to resonate especially widely and eventually gave birth to the Black Lives Matter movement. After Brown was killed, Obama was, initially, relatively quiet. As the protests and demonstrations spread, the administration dispatched Justice Department officials to Ferguson and closely monitored the demonstrations and riots that followed the shooting. But Obama deliberately avoided saying anything about the specifics of the case.

"I urge everyone in Ferguson, Missouri, and across the country, to remember this young man through reflection and understanding," Obama said days after the shooting. "We should comfort each other and talk with one another in a way that heals, not in a way that wounds."

Obama's distance drew scorn from critics on the left, who thought he should be leading the conversation about police brutality. Detractors on the right portrayed the president and Attorney General Eric H. Holder Jr. as "anti-cop" crusaders. In November, after a grand jury declined to indict Wilson in the shooting, Obama went to the White House briefing room at 10 p.m. to urge calm. The address was carried live on cable news as a split screen showed police cars burning in Ferguson.

"We need to recognize that the situation in Ferguson speaks to broader challenges that we still face as a nation. The fact is, in too many parts of this country, a deep distrust exists between law enforcement and communities of color. Some of this is the result of the legacy of racial discrimination in this country. And this is tragic, because nobody needs good policing more than poor communities with higher crime rates."

But in the months between Brown's death and Wilson's non-indictment, the frustration on the streets had begun to crystallize into a larger protest movement. It was a coalition made up of young black and brown activist groups that had formed after other racially charged incidents during the Obama years: the deaths of Jordan Davis and Oscar Grant, in addition to those of Martin and Garner. These groups took to the streets in dozens of cities to assert that "black lives matter," in what was soon being declared a new social justice movement.

On Dec. 1, 2014, Obama announced he would host several of the most active Ferguson protesters in the White House, a meeting which was the first of several coming signals that the White House stood behind the tenets of the protest movement. Obama would spend much of 2015 declaring criminal justice issues as among his primary priorities.

In addition to the policing question, Obama focused on disparities in sentencing, particularly in drug cases. Holder said Obama saw the racial disparity of the decades-long war on drugs close up when he was a community organizer on the South Side of Chicago.

During his second year in office, Obama signed the Fair Sentencing Act. The law reduced the disparity in the penalties for crack and powder cocaine, which civil rights leaders had said for years unfairly punished African Americans.

Under the old law a person convicted of possessing five grams of crack cocaine, which is cheaper and more available in poor black communities, received a mandatory five-year prison sentence. But someone who possessed powder cocaine, used by more affluent whites, had to be holding 100 times that amount to get the same mandatory sentence. The new law narrowed that ratio from 100 to 1 to about 18 to 1. Sentencing reform advocates would like him to close the gap further.

And overall, the results have been mixed. Many prosecutors are continuing to resist changes to mandatory minimum sentencing, and the administration's initiatives have not made a significant dent in the number of inmates crowded into federal prisons.

In the key executive action that Obama can take to undo unfair sentences, he has granted clemency to 248 federal inmates. White House Counsel Neil Eggleston said that Obama has commuted the sentences of more people than the past five presidents combined and that "we expect that the president will grant more commutations and pardons to deserving individuals in his final year in office."

But sentencing reform advocates have complained about the slow and cumbersome clemency process. They say that Obama raised hopes and expectations of all the federal inmates who meet the criteria established by the Justice Department but has not delivered for them.

CHAPTER 3

COMMANDER IN CHIEF

Obama as commander in chief:
Two experts offer opposing views

Read two takes on Obama's effectiveness as commander in chief, starting with "Obama's weak words of war" by Eliot A. Cohen.

Obama's weak words of war
By Eliot A. Cohen

Eliot A. Cohen, a former member of the George W. Bush administration, is the author of "Supreme Command: Soldiers, Statesmen, and Leadership in Wartime." He teaches at Johns Hopkins University.

Barack Obama may not have envisioned himself as a wartime commander in chief in 2008, but that is what he inevitably became — as was his predecessor, as will be his successor. He will be faulted for many things in this role, no doubt, but one of the weightiest criticisms is, on its surface, the least probable for this rhetorically gifted man: his failures of speech.

A wartime political leader has to do many things — order operations, approve plans, appoint and dismiss generals. Obama has done all of these things, some difficult (deciding to relieve Gen. Stanley A. McChrystal in Afghanistan), others perhaps less so (ordering the raid that killed Osama bin Laden). But he or she must also speak — clearly and persuasively — to foreign populations and domestic legislators, to the troops, to allied leaders, even to implacable enemies.

Obama has not explained to the American people, and certainly not at any length, the reasons he has continued the wars in Afghanistan and Iraq, rather than bringing them to an end as he had promised. He has declared wars won (against al-Qaeda) when they were anything but. He has dismissed those who disagree with him on questions about the use of force as either warmongers or hopelessly naive. He has painted the picture of a future without nuclear weapons while the arsenals of hostile nuclear powers have grown.

The president has dismissed as folly the notion of arming Syrian rebels — before arming them — and diagnosed a quagmire for Russia in the Middle East when, in fact, it is extending its power and reach. He has conducted the most extensive campaign of assassination (targeted killing, if one prefers) in the history of war, without adequately making the difficult case for it, even as he has suggested that Americans' fears of terrorism are vastly overblown.

Absence of speech, vain speech, erroneous speech — what explains it? Obama is, after all, no pacifist, and he is not squeamish. Someone who has ordered the third Iraq war in a quarter-century, a profusion of drone strikes and commando raids, intervention in Libya, an upgraded presence in Europe and provocative (but necessary) naval patrols in the South China Sea is hardly squeamish.

He has been crippled in part by his repugnance for the role. The dark secret of many successful wartime leaders is that, in some ways, they enjoy it: They like the company of soldiers; they are braced by the challenges of exercising power; they even seek some measure of martial glory. To many of us, that zest for the conduct of war is repulsive, but it is part of what lured Abraham Lincoln to the front lines and Franklin Roosevelt to his map room; it is what kept Winston Churchill growling from the rooftop of the prime minister's residence during the bombing of London.

For Obama, on the other hand, the orchestration of armed force is utterly inglorious. The men and women who wage war on behalf of the United States merit respect and, indeed, admiration, but perhaps more so solicitude and even pity. In the game of international politics, he seems to disdain the challenges of a cold-eyed realpolitiker like Vladimir Putin, thinking of the Russian leader's

President Obama speaks to military personnel at Camp Victory in Baghdad in April 2007. (Charles Dharapak/Associated Press)

Obama and Russian President Vladimir Putin toast at a luncheon during the United Nations General Assembly in New York in 2015. (Amanda Voisard/United Nations via Associated Press)

Obama, along with Vice President Biden, then-Secretary of State Hillary Clinton and members of the national security team, receives an update on the mission against Osama bin Laden on May 1, 2011. (Pete Souza/White House via Associated Press)

version of "Game of Thrones" as a distasteful and absurd activity, ultimately as unimportant as it is unpleasant.

For Obama, it's more about the G-20 than NATO, more about domestic societal reforms than the contest for international power or the struggle against an implacable foe. Libya, Ukraine and Syria are ugly distractions from the business of building a more perfect republic at home.

Arrogance is the other, and deeper, reason for Obama's failed speech as commander in chief. In the now notorious interview with Jeffrey Goldberg in the Atlantic, he makes clear his contempt for opinions, with regard to national security, other than his own and those of a few subordinates. He is right, self-evidently and obviously, and if others are too obtuse or malicious to understand, so much the worse for them. No need to persuade or explain.

Elections have consequences, after all, and he won two decisively, and would win a third against any conceivable challenger, or so he believes. Worse yet, arrogance leads to misjudgment of others. The world of war yields constant surprises — we now learn that bin Laden, for example, was not, as was claimed shortly after his death, out of touch with his subordinates and dejected about Arab politics. Iran is not particularly interested in cooperation with the United States in the Middle East. Iraq was not in adequate shape to be left to its own devices. But if you are convinced that you know better than foreign leaders, domestic rivals and experts of every type, always have and always will, what is the point of talk?

Now more than ever, we need a president who can speak to the American people about national security — someone who can explain the generational conflict with jihadis; the dangers a revanchist Russia poses in Europe; the no-less-fraught rise of Chinese military power and claims in Asia; why we should care about a Middle East whose violence never stays contained there; why we have to continue to fight the Taliban; why our alliances matter, to include the commitment to wage war. The old consensus on the use of military force is crumbling; we need someone to rebuild it and that can only be done by someone eloquently talking us through the complexity. It's a pity that for the last eight years a more-than-usually-fluent president has failed to do so.

The long game vs. the long war
By Derek Chollet

Derek Chollet, a former Pentagon official in the Obama administration, is counselor and senior adviser for security and defense policy at the German Marshall Fund of the United States. His book, "The Long Game: How Obama Defied Washington and Redefined America's Role in the World," will be published this month.

Although he never saw battle or served in uniform, Barack Obama entered the White House with bold ambitions for what he wanted to achieve as commander in chief.

Instead of thinking about the U.S. role in the world in terms of military might alone — what in the post-9/11 years became known as fighting the "long war" — Obama sought to forge a grand strategy that reflects the totality of American interests and to project global leadership in an era of seemingly infinite demands and finite resources. This is playing the "long game."

Obama sees war for what it is: often necessary, but always tragic. In his 2009 Nobel Peace Prize speech, which remains Obama's most important statement on the use of force, he made clear that the "instruments of war" are indispensable to the preservation of peace. He is willing to pull the trigger — think the Afghanistan surge in 2009, the bin Laden raid, hundreds of counterterrorism operations with drones or special operations forces, or the nearly 10,000 airstrikes against the Islamic State in Iraq and Syria since 2014. But at the same time, Obama often said privately that he did not want "killing people" to be his only lasting legacy.

At the core of moving from the long war to the long game is how one defines strength. Obama is frustrated that in the minds of many, military might is seen as the only meaningful metric of strength and leadership. He believes that too often the Washington debate defines strength simply as bold action with military might, and acting in the name of being "tough." As Obama explained in a news conference late last year: "American strength and American exceptionalism is not just a matter of us bombing somebody."

Obama's effort to recalibrate the instruments of American power has led to tensions with some military leaders; the intense debates over the surge in Afghanistan and the pace of the withdrawal in Iraq (and later, what to do about Libya and Syria) strained these relationships even further. But while they could be volatile, they were hardly broken. In fact, as I saw first-hand, Obama's relationships with his military leaders were for the most part strong and, with many of them, personally warm. He and his closest advisers took great care to tend to civil-military relations. And during the course of his presidency, Obama forged close bonds with his top military commanders, especially those such as Army Gen. Martin Dempsey, chairman of the Joint Chiefs of Staff from 2011 through 2015, who was perceived by the White House as an astute straight shooter.

Yet there is a natural tension between what the military demands in resources and what political leaders are ready to provide. There is also a fine line between civilians asking questions for greater specificity about military planning or fine-tuning options (to ensure they do not extend beyond the stated goals), and meddling in military decision-making. Obama appreciated the fundamental difference of perspectives, often saying that he understood why military commanders asked for the resources they did, but that his job was to consider such requests in the overall context of other interests, competing priorities and the trade-offs between them.

Sometimes the heat of debate would cause these differences to boil over. The second Afghanistan policy review in 2009 is an example. Numerous press leaks about the troop numbers Pentagon leaders were requesting caused frustrations in the White House that the military was "jamming" the president by raising the costs

Cadets at West Point gather in December 2009 for a speech by Obama, in which he outlined his plan to send tens of thousands of additional troops to Afghanistan. (Chris Hondros/Getty Images)

for him of "rejecting" their advice and, in effect, reducing his options (Obama certainly believed this to be the case). Intentional or not, such leaks accentuated these inherent tensions, leading to the impression that civil-military relations were more troubled than they actually were. Yet this was hardly the same kind of bitter struggle that plagued the George W. Bush administration, when the epic "generals' revolt" over the direction of the Iraq war exploded in public in 2006, a factor that ultimately led to the dismissal of Defense Secretary Donald H. Rumsfeld.

The key premise behind Obama's shift from the long war to the long game was simple common sense: Even when America is most powerful, there are constraints on what it can do. And that's why it cannot overextend itself, especially militarily.

This sense of restraint is difficult to communicate without being criticized for being defeatist or for denying America's inherent greatness. Obama often rejected the criticism that acknowledging limits was somehow new.

One of Obama's fundamental challenges as commander in chief was being forced to conduct a long-game strategy in a political and policy ecosystem that increasingly has come to resemble a reality television show with all the characteristics of professional wrestling: This new dynamic rewards over-the-top rhetoric and concocted drama instead of results that can be truly appreciated only with time.

When describing America's role in the world, Obama has often pledged that the "tide of war is receding." He has also frequently declared the war in Iraq as over and committed to bring the U.S. military role in Afghanistan to an end. So as American military forces returned to Iraq in 2014 and intensive U.S. airstrikes continued, many argued that Obama had finally been mugged by reality.

Considering the scope and scale of America's current military campaign against the Islamic State in Iraq, Syria and elsewhere, it is true the tide of war is still with us. In retrospect, some of Obama's declarative rhetoric suggested starker conclusions than actually existed. Each day, thousands of U.S. military personnel take the fight to the Islamic State, whether by conducting direct military action or by supporting partners and allies on the ground, often at great risk. Given that Obama's strategy is premised on sustainability and patience, this battle will be conducted far into the future. He has always been clear about that fact.

This is where Obama as commander in chief is misunderstood — and, by some, purposely misportrayed. He has never believed in complete U.S. withdrawal from the Middle East or renounced the importance of military power. In words and actions, Obama has made clear his commitment to America's interests and partners in the region, and to defeating the Islamic State. But he is equally determined not to ruin the country in the process or let the problems of the Middle East become the singular obsession of American foreign policy. In this sense, while Obama remains a president at war, he is not a "war president," in which all other aspects of his foreign policy are subsumed by his use of military force.

When explaining his decisions to use force, Obama explicitly stresses the attributes of balance, precision and sustainability, explaining his choices in the context of addressing other priorities at home and abroad. Obama is fond of quoting Eisenhower's adage about national security decisions, saying that "each proposal must be weighed in the light of a broader consideration: the need to maintain balance in and among national programs."

This weighing of ends and means, calibrating an approach within the context of the totality of American interests, is the essence of grand strategy. The military aspects could not be open-ended or considered in isolation. For Obama, the key is not to allow the long war to return as the organizing principle for America in the world, causing everything else — our other interests, our values, our resource decisions — to be swallowed up. This fight must always be waged in the context of the long game.

For one Washington Post staff writer — a Marine infantryman at the time — the surge in Afghanistan was personal

Before attending Georgetown University and becoming a Washington Post staff writer, Thomas Gibbons-Neff served with the 1st Battalion, 6th Marine Regiment from 2007 to 2011 as an infantryman. He deployed twice to Afghanistan — in 2008 and 2009 — where he led a small team during Operation Moshtarak, the mission to retake the city of Marja in Helmand province from the Taliban, in February 2010. The joint U.S.-Afghan mission was the largest of its kind since the start of the war, and Gibbons-Neff's team accompanied 120 Marines of 1/6's Bravo Company into the heart of the city.

In the ensuing weeks, the Marines of Bravo Company cleared large portions of the city after facing heavy Taliban resistance. Although some of the fighting would drop off in the following months, the Taliban remained a persistent threat even after the Marines of 1/6 left in July 2010.

Feb. 14, 2010: U.S. soldiers and one Afghan soldier exchanged fire with insurgents in support of the Marine offensive against the Taliban in the Marja area. In that fight, one soldier was wounded and at least one insurgent was killed. (Pier Paolo Cito/Associated Press)

Feb. 14, 2010: As the battle for Marja unfolded, Bravo Company found itself surrounded and in need of additional support. Charlie Company, part of the 1st Battalion 6th Marine Regiment, and its complement of vehicles headed toward Bravo Company to lend that support. (Andrea Bruce for The Washington Post)

Feb. 15, 2010: After an intense firefight in which many Marines were wounded, the regiment's commander, at right, paid a visit to the temporary headquarters of Bravo Company. Cpl. Thomas Gibbons-Neff, left, had just come off the roof of the building, where a Marine had been shot through his helmet. (Andrea Bruce for The Washington Post)

March 2, 2010: During a helicopter medical evacuation by the Army's 82nd Airborne Division, known as Task Force Pegasus, flight medic Sgt. Bryan Eickelberg secured a tarp around the body of an Afghan National Army soldier killed in Marja minutes earlier in an improvised explosive device attack. Pegasus crews provided the fast medical evacuation of seriously wounded combatants and civilians, and also transported those killed in action. (Brennan Linsley/Associated Press)

March 26, 2010: A member of the 3rd Battalion, 6th Marine Regiment held the dog tag of a fallen comrade as he paid his final respects during a memorial ceremony for four fallen comrades at their base in Marja. (Mauricio Lima/Agence France-Presse via Getty Images)

May 31, 2010: A Marine took a break behind his vehicle at Forward Operating Base Marja, which was the hub for most operations in the southern portion of the city. By the end of the 1st Battalion 6th Marines Regiment's deployment, the base had a chow hall and air-conditioned tents for the Marines based there. (Andrea Bruce for The Washington Post)

June 4, 2010: Marines in Marja often executed their patrols in flooded ditches, or wadis, to avoid the many improvised explosive devices buried in the roads and trails. (Andrea Bruce for The Washington Post)

Sept. 24, 2010: Army flight medic Sgt. Tyrone Jordan, attached to Dustoff Task Force Shadow of the 101st Combat Aviation Brigade, carried Marine Lance Cpl. David Hawkins to a medical helicopter after he was wounded by a blast from an IED in Marja. Task Force Shadow was responsible for evacuating wounded forces, as well as locals, throughout southern Afghanistan. (Scott Olson/Getty Images)

A wartime president struggles with the hard questions

By Greg Jaffe

In February 2009, less than two months after he took office, President Obama had flew to Camp Lejeune, N.C., and laid out his plan for ending the war in Iraq. He stood surrounded by camouflage-clad Marines, many of whom were just days away from being shipped off to Iraq or Afghanistan.

"Next month will mark the sixth anniversary of the war in Iraq," Obama told the troops. "By any measure, this has already been a long war."

Obama rose to national prominence in 2002 on the eve of the Iraq invasion by calling it a "dumb war; a rash war; a war based not on reason, but on passion; not on principle, but on politics." His candidacy hinged on his promise to end it as quickly as possible.

He was far from the first person to wrestle with the question of how to bring the messy, grinding fight to a close. In March 2003, with American troops bogged down by guerilla attacks on the way to Baghdad, then-Maj. Gen. David H. Petraeus turned to a reporter and uttered one of the most prescient sentences of the Iraq war: "Tell me how this ends."

President Bush thought he had his answer — the "Mission Accomplished" moment — on the aircraft carrier USS Abraham Lincoln two months later, shortly after the fall of Saddam Hussein. "Because of you, our nation is more secure," he told the sailors on the Lincoln. "Because of you, the tyrant has fallen, and Iraq

70

is free." But the war would consume Bush for the remainder of his presidency.

Obama followed Bush into the White House determined not to let his presidency be defined by war — especially not the one in Iraq, which had already cost more than 4,000 American lives and tens of thousands of Iraqi lives, when he took office.

His plans to end the conflict, though, have been undone by Iraq's poisonous sectarian politics, Iranian meddling, his own mistakes and the devastating civil war across the border in Syria. Like Petraeus, he struggled to answer that most fundamental of questions: "Tell me how this ends."

At Camp Lejeune, Obama sketched out one answer, telling the Marines that they had "fought against tyranny and disorder." They had bled for their "best friends and for unknown Iraqis." They had "served with honor."

But they could not do the job of diplomats and civilian advisers who would stay behind after the troops came home to help the Iraqis forge a lasting peace. "We'll help Iraqis strengthen institutions that are just, representative and accountable," Obama promised. "We'll build new ties of trade and of commerce, culture and education, that unleash the potential of the Iraqi people."

But the final hours of the American occupation suggested a very different end.

We expect our wars to end in iconic moments. Gen. Robert E. Lee's surrender at Appomattox in 1865; the 1945 Life magazine photo of a sailor planting a kiss on an unsuspecting woman in Times Square; a helicopter frantically evacuating U.S. personnel from a CIA annex in Saigon in 1975.

"It's harder to end a war than begin one," Obama told troops at Fort Bragg on Dec. 14, 2011. He was right in a way he never anticipated.

The next day the American military's top brass gathered at Baghdad International Airport to mark what was supposed to be the end of the war. Defense Secretary Leon E. Panetta offered up the usual praise for the troops. Gen. Lloyd Austin, who had pressed to keep a force of as many as 15,000 American troops in the country, gave a half-hearted endorsement to the proceedings, pronouncing Iraq a "relatively peaceful environment."

The Iraqis offered up the ceremony's most powerful statement by refusing at the last minute to attend. Just before the ceremony was to start, an American soldier was dispatched to snatch the placards reserving seats in the front row for then-Iraqi Prime Minister Nouri al-Maliki and the top members of his cabinet.

Two days later, the last American troops gathered at Contingency Operating Base Adder for the final convoy out of Iraq. At its peak, the base held more than 12,000 American troops and contractors, a Taco Bell, a movie theater and six bus routes.

The Americans were leaving behind 500 pickup trucks, buses and cars in the base motor pool, with the keys on the dashboards. "This place is going to be like Black Friday at Wal-Mart when we leave," joked an Iraqi American interpreter.

Iraq's problems were evident, even to a casual observer. A six-man Iraqi band, dressed in dirty blue uniforms, played a ragged marching song on dented trumpets and trombones as the Americans and Iraqis signed the final paperwork handing over the facility, which the Iraqis had renamed Imam Ali Air Base. Its only plane was a rusty, white passenger aircraft with no landing gear and a broken propeller.

The U.S. military flew in a gaggle of television reporters a few hours before the final convoy left for Kuwait. Geraldo Rivera, the Fox News personality and future "Dancing With the Stars" contestant, posed for pictures with the American soldiers. Some troops cooked hamburgers and hot dogs on a grill fashioned out of a steel barrel.

The Americans finally left the base about 3 a.m., rolling out under the cover of darkness as drones and attack helicopters circled protectively overhead.

The day after the Americans had cleared the border, Maliki's Shiite-dominated government issued an arrest warrant for Iraq's Sunni vice president, beginning a sectarian cleansing that would

U.S. soldiers train Iraqi forces in a live-fire exercise in Basmaya, southeast of Baghdad, in January 2016. (Ahmad al-Rubaye/Agence France-Presse via Getty Images)

tear the country apart. In 2014, when the Iraqi army collapsed and the Islamic State swept through Iraq's majority Sunni provinces, the Obama administration blamed Maliki for gutting the government and the military. Republicans blamed Obama for not pressing harder to keep an American force in the country. Senior military officials — many of whom believed that they had salvaged something close to victory by 2011 — blamed the political leadership in Washington for letting things spiral out of control in Iraq after the last troops left.

Obama responded to the Islamic State advance by sending in fighter jets, bombers and 475 military advisers. Today, the number of U.S. troops in Iraq is 5,000, and it is almost certain to grow. As Obama's presidency draws to a close, he still struggles to define victory in a place like Iraq. In December 2015, after terrorist attacks in Paris and San Bernardino, Calif., Obama took another cut at it in a prime-time Oval Office address.

Victory was not getting sucked back into a "long and costly ground war in Iraq or Syria," he said. "That's what groups like ISIL want," he said, using another name for the Islamic State. It had less to do with what actually happened on the ground in Iraq and Syria than how Americans reacted at home.

Instead of answering Petraeus's question, Obama sought to flip it.

"Let's make sure we never forget what makes us exceptional," Obama said from the White House as he prepared to enter the final year of his presidency. "Let's not forget that freedom is more powerful than fear."

From Syria to San Bernardino, the rise of the Islamic State remakes the terrorism equation

By Missy Ryan

The 2011 uprising against President Bashar al-Assad spawned a violent, multisided conflict in Syria. As a result, opposition fighters claimed vast tracts of the country, allowing an array of armed groups space to gain strength.

As Syria's civil war grew more complex, the remnants of a group once known as al-Qaeda in Iraq moved into Syria and became a powerful force among opposition groups. The Islamic State became known for its success in recruiting foreign fighters and for its zealous imposition of sharia law in the areas it captures.

In early 2014, Islamic State fighters took control of the city of Fallujah in western Iraq, revealing the fragility of Iraq's security only two years after the departure of U.S. troops. Six months later, Islamic State militants streamed into northern Iraq and captured Mosul, Iraq's second-largest city, taking the government in Baghdad and its western backers by surprise. The Islamic State's advance was made possible by the collapse of Iraqi army units stationed around Mosul, raising questions about earlier U.S. efforts to build an effective military force in Iraq.

The arrival of the Islamic State proved calamitous for minorities in northern Iraq. The Islamic State executed Yazidis around the town of Sinjar; others faced harrowing conditions when they fled to nearby mountains. The United States launched its first airstrikes against the Islamic State, around Sinjar and in protection of the Kurdish capital, Irbil, in August 2014.

Free Syria Army fighters battle with regime loyalist soldiers in Aleppo, Syria, in 2012. (Javier Manzano/ Agence France-Presse via Getty Images)

Two Syrian rebels take sniper positions in central Aleppo in 2012. (Javier Manzano/Agence France-Presse via Getty Images)

Yazidis cross a bridge from Syria back into Iraq in 2014. (Sebastian Meyer for The Washington Post)

People hold a photograph of James Foley during a memorial service in Irbil, Iraq, in August 2014. (Marko Drobnjakovic/Associated Press)

An explosion rocks Kobani, Syria, during an attack by Islamic State militants in 2014. (Gokhan Sahin/ Getty Images)

A family in Evzoni, Greece, heads toward the Macedonian border in May 2015. (Charles Ommanney for The Washington Post)

Footage from a helmet camera shows U.S. and Iraqi special forces freeing hostages from an Islamic State-controlled prison in Iraq in October 2015. (Associated Press)

A man wrapped in a Belgian flag joins others at a makeshift memorial in front of Brussels's Stock Exchange after the attacks in March. (Philippe Huguen/ Agence France-Presse via Getty Images)

Tashfeen Malik, left, and her husband, Syed Farook — the couple who carried out the attack in San Bernardino, Calif. — pass through Chicago O'Hare International Airport in July 2014. (U.S. Customs and Border Protection via Associated Press)

The Islamic State began to execute foreign hostages it held in Syria, including American journalists James Foley and Steven Sotloff. The killings galvanized public sentiment against the Islamic State. The next month, the Obama administration and its partners broadened their campaign of airstrikes to Syria.

President Obama authorized the return of substantial numbers of U.S. military personnel to Iraq for the first time since the 2011 withdrawal. American advisers were tasked with helping to rebuild a capable military force that can dislodge the Islamic State.

U.S. strikes helped partner forces in Iraq and Syria make limited gains against the Islamic State. In Syria, Kurdish forces took back control of Kobani, a city on the Turkish border. In Iraq, government forces pushed into the militant-held city of Tikrit.

Harsh conditions in areas under Islamic State control swelled the flows of migrants heading for Europe, exposing divisions among the 28-member European Union and heightening fears about militant attacks there.

The Obama administration gradually expanded its military role on the ground in a bid to accelerate progress against the Islamic State. While the White House insisted that U.S. troops would not take part in combat operations, troops helped local forces conduct dangerous operations. The first combat death occurred in October 2015, when American Special Operations forces accompanied Kurdish pershmerga troops on a hostage raid.

The reach of the Islamic State beyond Iraq and Syria became starkly clear when militants launched a series of coordinated attacks across Paris in November 2015, killing at least 130 people.

New attacks on the Brussels airport and metro system in March 2016 further illustrated the vulnerability of European nations to home-grown militant plots.

Although the United States has been shielded from the bulk of Europeans' fears about migrant-related security threats, its own vulnerability was exposed in December 2015, when two California residents, voicing loyalty to the Islamic State, launched an attack on a gathering of municipal workers, killing 14 people and wounding at least 22 more. The attack, the deadliest terrorist attack on U.S. soil since Sept. 11, 2001, triggered an ongoing controversy about the limits of government access to personal data and the role of Muslim immigrants in the United States.

With his reliance on drones, Obama embraced a deadly, high-altitude, secretive war

By Greg Miller

Barack Obama was supposed to be the president who reined in the CIA. In campaign speeches, he had sharply criticized the agency's approach against al-Qaeda. The first orders he signed as president closed the CIA's overseas prisons and banned its brutal interrogation methods. Many agency employees braced for a sustained assault on authorities that had only expanded since the Sept. 11 attacks.

But on Jan. 23, 2009 — Obama's third day in office — a Predator drone flying over Pakistan released a Hellfire missile that slammed into a suspected Taliban compound, killing 18 people inside.

The CIA strike was the first of more than 500 that would take place over the next eight years, a campaign that, according to most estimates, has killed at least 3,000 militants and hundreds of civilians. For all he did to check the CIA's powers, Obama will more likely be remembered as the president who unleashed the agency's fleet of armed drones.

Obama inherited that lethal capability, which the agency had initially developed to target Osama bin Laden, and then employed it sporadically as it scoured Pakistan's tribal belt for senior al-Qaeda operatives. But the program expanded under Obama's watch in important and sometimes initially invisible ways.

The pace of the campaign's strikes in Pakistan surged from several dozen in 2008 to 117 in Obama's second year.

The acceleration was enabled by Obama's secret embrace of a controversial tactic known as "signature strikes," which meant the CIA could fire at suspicious gatherings of suspected militants without actually knowing who they were.

The program also spread geographically, as the agency added drone bases in Saudi Arabia, Turkey and other locations, platforms still being used for both armed and unarmed flights over conflicts in Yemen and Syria.

As a result, Obama came to be branded as the drone president long before he could bring himself to publicly utter the word.

That didn't happen until 2013, when Obama delivered a long-awaited speech at the National Defense University on counterterrorism policy and acknowledged — awkwardly — the existence of "remotely piloted aircraft commonly referred to as drones."

That a former constitutional law professor would come to rely so heavily on an unprecedented — and critics argued extrajudicial — program of targeted killings was a source of tension that Obama seemed to struggle with throughout his tenure.

Even while touting drones' accuracy and effectiveness in that National Defense University speech, Obama expressed concern about the seductive appeal of a program that enables a commander in chief to eliminate U.S. adversaries without putting any American lives at risk or subjecting the covert capability to public scrutiny.

"The very precision of drone strikes and the necessary secrecy often involved in such actions can end up shielding our government from the public scrutiny that a troop deployment invites," Obama said. "It can also lead a president and his team to view drone strikes as a cure-all for terrorism."

Obama sought repeatedly to address the accountability issue. His national security team spent much of his first term developing a counterterrorism playbook designed to impose tighter rules on drone strikes, detailing the criteria for selecting targets and specifying the White House or CIA approvals required before a Hellfire missile could be fired.

The White House released white papers summarizing the secret memos that served as the drone program's legal foundation, seeking to assure the public that strikes were permitted only on suspected terrorists who posed an "imminent threat" and only when capture was not feasible.

Although welcomed by civil liberties groups, the administration's measures never succeeded in quieting critics who continued to see CIA drone operations as excessively secretive, legally dubious and tactically counterproductive.

The rise of the Islamic State terror group in Syria and the resilience of al-Qaeda appeared to have only added to Obama's warning that drone strikes should not be considered "a cure-all for terrorism."

CHAPTER 4

OBAMA'S AMERICA

Obama rescued the economy.
Could he have done more?

By Benjamin M. Friedman

On March 4, 1933, at the bottom of the worst financial and economic crisis to afflict the United States since the Civil War, Franklin D. Roosevelt took office as president. Two days later, Roosevelt acted to stanch the collapse by suspending gold payments, imposing a four-day "bank holiday" and arranging emergency assistance for banks when they reopened.

Over the next three months — FDR's legendary "100 days" — the new administration initiated further measures, including federal job creation, welfare relief, aid to homeowners unable to pay their mortgages, and securities and banking reform. By the end of Roosevelt's first term, the list of fundamental and lasting innovations, all responses to the crisis, included unemployment insurance, Social Security and the Federal Deposit Insurance Corp.

Barack Obama took office Jan. 20, 2009, during the worst financial and economic crisis since World War II. By then, the Federal Reserve System had already acted to prevent the collapse of the banking system, and so the new president moved forward promptly to spur the depressed economy. The fiscal package he signed Feb. 17, 2009, allocated $787 billion — more than 5 percent of a year's total U.S. income — to infrastructure investment, job training, aid to low-income workers, tax relief in various forms and other measures aimed at stimulating economic activity. The money could have been better directed, so as to achieve greater impact, and in retrospect the amount was too small. But in the face of opposition from Republicans in Congress, Obama's fiscal stimulus was about as much as any president could have done.

After pushing through the stimulus, however, the Obama administration entered a period of quietude on the economic front. Despite large Democratic majorities in both houses of Congress, there was no other significant economic legislation during the new president's first 100 days. Nor in the 100 days following that, nor in the 100 days after that.

Financial reforms to prevent a repeat of the disaster that had just happened were on hold. The administration took no advantage of the potential leverage the government had gained through its infusion of taxpayer money to recapitalize banks that would otherwise have failed. (By spring 2009, the U.S. Treasury owned 38 percent of the equity in Citibank.) Other potential economic policy initiatives, such as tax reform, remained out of sight.

Instead, once the economic stimulus became law, the Obama domestic agenda shifted to health care. When the president took office, roughly one in six Americans — 50 million in a population of 307 million — had no health insurance. The Affordable Care Act, passed in March 2010, has now provided coverage to 20 million of those 50 million. If more states expanded Medicare, as was permitted under the new law and clearly expected by Obama, the number would be significantly greater. Moreover, some of the 30 million remaining uncovered are in the United States illegally and are therefore ineligible.

Raising the insured total to more than 90 percent of all Americans will likely stand as a historic achievement, but the cost was a diversion of the administration's energy and attention from other economic problems badly in need of remedy.

The most pressing among them was, and remains, financial reform. Rather than advance its own set of proposals — especially during the president's first year in office, when the Democrats held a filibuster-proof supermajority in the Senate — the administration largely left the matter to Congress.

The result, the Dodd-Frank Act, passed in July 2010, represented a reasonable first pass at fixing a dangerously defective financial system. Among other useful contributions, the new legislation called for higher bank capital requirements; strengthened procedures for resolving the failure of banks and other financial companies; restricted banks' latitude to invest in risky securities; and established a new, centralized mechanism for trading some of the financial derivative instruments that had been at the center of the crisis.

By contrast, some of the act's provisions, most importantly the weakened ability of the Federal Reserve and the FDIC to rescue banks in any future crisis, may well prove counterproductive.

Overall, if Dodd-Frank were merely one in a series of financial reform packages aimed at addressing what had happened from 2007 to 2009, it would have been a laudable first step. But as the nation's principal response to the worst financial crisis in two generations, it paled. Further, the specifics of many of the intended reforms were left to agency-level rulemaking exercises — at one point more than 300 of them were in process — that, predictably, enabled industry lobbyists to blunt their force, if not thwart them altogether.

As the crisis and its immediate aftermath receded, the Obama administration's economic policy agenda shifted to mostly defensive actions domestically, combined with negotiating what have proved to be highly controversial trade agreements abroad. The main achievement of the intensely political 2011 budget deal with the by-now-Republican House of Representatives was simply to avoid the U.S. government's defaulting on its debt. In 2013, the president succeeded in increasing the tax rate for top-bracket earners from 35 percent back to 39.6 percent, where it had been in the Clinton years; in exchange, he agreed to extend, indefinitely, the rest of the Bush administration's 2003 cuts for taxpayers with annual earnings of up to $450,000 per couple. (Later in 2013, in the course of a further dispute over budgets and debt, House Republicans shut down the government for 17 days.)

The president also pressed forward with two large-scale trade agreements: the Transatlantic Trade and Investment Partnership (TTIP), between the United States and the European Union, and the Trans-Pacific Partnership (TPP), with most of the major Pacific nations other than China. If implemented, these agreements would lower tariffs, remove various other trade barriers, and make cross-border investment easier and safer. Whether they will ever take effect, however, remains uncertain. As often happens when the economy stagnates, to many citizens free trade seems more a threat than an opportunity. Donald Trump made opposition to TPP a centerpiece of his presidential campaign, and Hillary Clinton, who supported TPP as secretary of state, now opposes it, as well.

The TTIP negotiations with the E.U. remain to be completed, so there is nothing for either candidate to oppose.

What remains for the next president to accomplish? During Obama's presidency, the country made little or no progress on long-standing issues such as tax reform and assuring the long-term viability of Medicare in the face of spiraling costs. The U.S. financial system remains too large, too expensive and too risky. Although Obama took some limited steps toward arresting the relentless widening of economic inequality — raising top-bracket tax rates, extending the earned-income tax credit and expanding the child tax credit, for example — the election campaign to replace him, in both parties, shows that the American public remains deeply unsatisfied.

Most important, the pace of improvement in America's productivity — how much the nation produces per person, or per worker, or per hour worked — has been slowing for the past four decades. With more rapid growth, many of today's economic challenges, especially widening inequality, would seem less worrisome. But with stagnating productivity, the resulting frustrations are rising toward boiling points. We know fairly little about how to boost an economy's productivity growth, although some identifiable measures would clearly help. Rebuilding the nation's physical infrastructure; restructuring education, especially in the early grades; providing prekindergarten to more "at risk" students;

and restoring the government's shrunken funding for research are all good choices. All cost money.

Obama made progress in some areas of economic policy, perhaps as much as the country's increasingly divided politics would allow, and on each of those fronts — economic and political — his successor will not lack for challenges.

Benjamin M. Friedman is the William Joseph Maier professor of political economy and former chairman of the Department of Economics at Harvard.

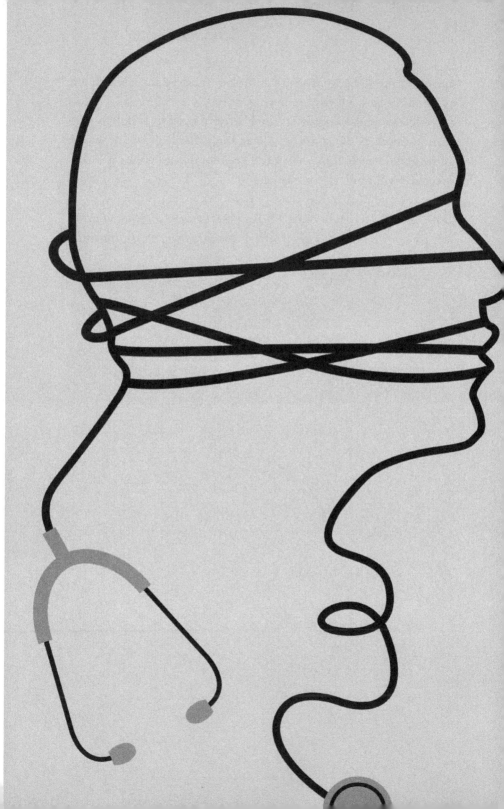

Obama's legislative legacy comes down to this question: What if?

By Mike DeBonis

In the moments before Barack Obama prepared to sign the health-care reform law that would forever define his domestic legacy, Joe Biden famously whispered into his ear: "This is a big [expletive] deal."

On that day, just 14 months into Obama's presidency, Biden could not know just how profoundly correct he was in that assessment.

One word — "Obamacare" — would come to represent the promise and the pitfalls of Obama's presidency. The March 2010 signing of the Patient Protection and Affordable Care Act stands as a pivot on which Obama's legislative agenda turned, where the audacity of hope gave way to the reality and frustrations of divided government.

Obama would sign only one more blockbuster policy bill — the Dodd-Frank financial reform law — which, together with Obamacare and the fiscal stimulus package he signed shortly after taking office, will share top billing in the legislative history of the Obama administration.

Instead, Democrats lost the House and later the Senate, and Obama spent the final six years of his presidency mired in a series of high-stakes negotiations focused soley on keeping the federal government open for business and preventing the country from defaulting on its debts.

Other major pieces of his legislative agenda — on climate

President Obama signs the Affordable Care Act in the East Room of the White House on March 23, 2010. (J. Scott Applewhite/Associated Press)

change, on immigration, on civil rights — stalled or died at different stages, and the administration turned to the exercise of executive power to achieve its goals.

"I've got a pen, and I've got a phone," he said in 2014, describing his levers of power as his dealings with Congress continued to deteriorate.

Thus, Obama's legislative legacy comes down to this question: What if?

Could health-care reform have been done in a different way? Could Democrats have kept control of Congress for another two years or more? Was Obamacare worth it?

The debate roiled Democrats, including some inside the administration, from the earliest days of the presidency. At the time, the nation remained beset by the economic turmoil sparked by the 2008 global financial meltdown, and many wondered whether health-care reform should be the top priority.

"I begged him not to do this," former chief of staff Rahm Emanuel told a reporter in 2010, airing his preference for a hard focus on jobs and the economy even after the passage of the stimulus bill.

On Capitol Hill, many Democratic lawmakers, aides and consultans wondered — openly and not — about the political costs of the dogged pursuit of health-care reform. The costs were to be measured not only in congressional seats but in policy priorities.

What would this mean for other major items on the Democratic agenda, ones requiring major outlays of presidential political capital? What about cap-and-trade, union "card check," the Dream Act or the Employment Non-Discrimination Act — each one a major priority for key parts of the Democratic base?

None of those bills would pass the 111th Congress, even though for the first time in more than 40 years one party held the presidency and dominant majorities in both houses of Congress.

'TOGETHER IN OPPOSITION'

The passage of the health-care law meant that, for the first time, Americans would be legally obligated to purchase insurance under the threat of tax penalties. In return, the law created new mechanisms to allow access to affordable insurance to millions who had been priced out of the market. New restrictions would keep employers and insurers from excluding the sick; a system of subsidized state exchanges would serve individuals without access to insurance through their jobs; and an expansion of Medicaid would cover a swath of Americans teetering above the poverty line.

Many of the ideas embedded in the law, including the individual mandate to buy insurance, had rattled around conservative think tank circles for decades as potential GOP alternatives to previous, more government-centric Democratic health-care plans.

But that history didn't forestall a furious partisan backlash — one that gave Republicans a crucial rallying point just months after the 2008 electoral rout. In his recent memoir, Senate Republican leader Mitch McConnell recalled his advice to his GOP colleagues: "Don't muddy this up."

"I didn't want a single Republican to vote for it," McConnell (Ky.) wrote. "It had to be very obvious to the voters which party was responsible for this terrible policy, and I wanted a clear line

Then-House Speaker Nancy Pelosi (D-Calif.) walks to the Capitol with Rep. John Lewis (D-Ga.), second from left, and others on March 21, 2010, ahead of a vote on the health-care law. (Melina Mara/The Washington Post)

Michelle Peele of College Park, Md., joins chants of "kill the bill" during a protest March 20, 2010. (Melina Mara/The Washington Post)

Then-House Minority Leader John A. Boehner (R-Ohio) speaks to then-Senate Minority Leader Mitch McConnell (R-Ky.) after a meeting March 18, 2010, on the health-care bill. (Melina Mara/The Washington Post)

of demarcation — they were for this, and we were against it. ... So the strategy, simply stated, was to keep everybody together in opposition."

The president craved the idea of a bipartisan bill, and Obama and congressional Democrats labored for months to get at least a few Republicans to buy in, soliciting input and suggestions from a few Republican senators, in particular. Ultimately, those talks went nowhere; every GOP senator agreed not to "muddy this up."

Meanwhile, the shoots of a grass-roots uprising began to show. What would become the tea party movement had started to coalesce in opposition to the financial recovery bills passed in the earliest months of Obama's presidency, and the health-care push gave it potent new fuel.

When the congressional summer recess came, protests erupted with chants of "kill the bill" in town hall meetings across the country.

"People are signaling that we ought to slow up and find out where we are and don't spend so much money and don't get us so far into debt," Sen. Charles E. Grassley (R-Iowa), one of three key Senate GOP negotiators, said that August after a pummeling series of home-state meetings. Lawmakers never came any closer to compromise.

The surprise victory the following January of a Republican, Scott Brown, in the Massachusetts special election to fill the seat of the late Sen. Edward M. Kennedy cemented the peril for Democrats — and for the president's agenda.

In a Washington Post op-ed days later, Obama political adviser David Plouffe acknowledged a "white-knuckled ride" ahead for his party's candidates but warned against "bed-wetting."

"I know that the short-term politics are bad," he said. "But politically speaking, if we do not pass it, the GOP will continue attacking the plan as if we did anyway, and voters will have no ability to measure its upside."

After a series of unusual legislative maneuvers and a flurry of intraparty deal-making, the Patient Protection and Affordable Care

Act passed Congress without the support of a single Republican lawmaker, and Obama signed it into law March 23, 2010. But the political consequences extended well beyond any definition of the short term.

VOWS TO REPEAL

The Republican vows to "repeal and replace" Obamacare began that very day — one that then-House Minority Leader John A. Boehner (R-Ohio) called "a somber day for the American people." Nine months later, he became the 53rd speaker of the House.

The GOP leveraged Obamacare into massive political gains, and they didn't end with the profound Democratic losses in the 2010 midterms. By the last year of the Obama administration, his party had lost 14 Senate seats, 68 House seats, 12 governorships and hundreds of state legislative seats.

One academic paper suggested that the Obamacare vote alone cost the Democrats roughly 25 House seats — the difference between a historic landslide and two more years in the majority.

The Senate remained under Democratic control until 2015, but a Republican House majority, with an ascendant cadre of hard-line tea party conservatives unwilling to compromise, meant that Obama's progressive agenda was a dead letter two years into his presidency.

Card check and cap-and-trade were out. A series of high-stakes fiscal cliffhangers were in, starting with a showdown over a potential U.S. credit default that ended in a deal forcing years of spending cuts that reined in Obama's domestic ambitions.

Fifteen years earlier, President Bill Clinton took his own mid-term lumps and proceeded to make a centrist peace with new GOP House Speaker Newt Gingrich (Ga.), cutting deals on welfare reform, crime and other bills. With the exception of a brief and unsuccessful attempt at a fiscal "grand bargain" in 2011, Obama did not seek compromise at a Clintonian scale — the gulf between his progressive agenda and a hard-right House majority was too wide, and seemingly unbridgeable.

When he did seek to push a controversial priority though Congress — notably, seeking to expand firearm background checks — he lost. Instead, he shifted his efforts away from a branch of government he did not control to the one he did. His domestic legacy would be written in policy memos and the obscure pages of federal agency rulemakings.

The Keystone XL pipeline would not be built; power plants would emit less carbon dioxide; investment advisers would adhere to higher standards; and environmental regulators would have new authority over U.S. waterways. The Obama administration did those things by itself over the loud objections of the Republican Congress.

Meanwhile, what Obama could accomplish by legislation lay in a few scant areas where he had significant agreement with Republican congressional leaders. And those have, by and large, failed to come to pass.

An attempt at the most ambitious immigration reform effort in decades had some early momentum in Obama's second term. Then an unknown college professor with an anti-immigration platform and tea-party support deposed the sitting House majority leader, Eric Cantor (Va.), in a little-noticed 2014 primary. Republicans were spooked, unwilling to move ahead. Obama responded with a new set of executive actions, further alienating Congress.

And his bid to ratify the Trans-Pacific Partnership trade agreement, the centerpiece of a foreign-policy "pivot to Asia," now appears dead on arrival thanks to grass-roots revolts in both parties. If the TPP moves forward, it will probably not be during Obama's presidency.

MIXED REVIEWS

Any reasonable analysis must conclude that the political opportunity costs of Obamacare have been considerable. The other side of the legacy ledger — the human benefits — are only beginning to be measured.

More Americans are insured than ever before, with federal data showing the uninsured rate dropping from 15 percent to 9 percent in the first three years of the law's implementation. Upwards of 20 million more Americans now have insurance, and the rise in health-care prices has slowed — although it is not clear how much can be directly attributed to the reform law.

Meanwhile, the long-term political benefits that Plouffe predicted have not materialized — far from it. Polls show a country sharply and continually divided on the law, largely along partisan lines.

A June 2016 survey from the Kaiser Family Foundation found that 29 percent of Americans say that Obamacare has hurt their family, compared to 18 percent who say it has helped. Most cited increased costs; others pointed to new difficulties in accessing care.

But Republicans faced political difficulties of their own. The party was consumed with attempts to repeal the law, even though another Kaiser poll found that only about a third of Americans favor a full repeal and about a third want to expand it. Polls also show voters still trust Democrats over Republicans to handle health care, although the margin has narrowed somewhat since Obamacare became law.

What congressional leaders never did, until way late in the game, was put forth a coherent alternative that attempts to address at least some of the gaps in the pre-Obamacare health system. And the sketch of an alternative released by House Republicans in summer 2015 presented no estimates of the plan's costs, nor did it lay out how many fewer Americans might be insured if their changes were implemented.

But the political calculus has been clear: Hard-line opposition has been awfully good for GOP candidates, even if the arguments don't always add up. McConnell, after describing how he forestalled any attempts at compromise, wrote in his memoir that the "chaos this law has visited on our country isn't just deeply tragic, it was entirely predictable."

He added: "That will always be the case if you approach legislation without regard for the views of the other side. Without some meaningful buy-in, you guarantee a food fight."

Even as Donald Trump's candidacy scrambled the GOP policy agenda, opposition to Obamacare remained near the top. "We are going to replace Obamacare with something so much better," said Trump, who has offered the barest outline of such a plan, in a February primary debate.

For Obama, the law has entered a mythic adolescence. The exhilaration of its passage and the frustration at its botched rollout have given way to a heroic narrative.

In a video aired before Obama's address to the Democratic National Convention this year, the passage of Obamacare took its place alongside his handling of the financial crisis and the killing of Osama bin Laden in a story about an embattled president's resolve to serve the American people. And Emanuel, the doubter, is the foil.

"He's thinking to himself, if I decide not to push forward, what do I say to all those people who came up to me with tears in their eyes telling me they need this to save themselves," former speechwriter Jon Favreau intones in a voice-over. "And if that means that I'm a one-term president, then I'm a one-term president."

He was not, in the end, a one-term president. But his decision carries a more complicated accounting. Given all the chaos, Obamacare may or may not have been the smart play at the time, but it was most certainly a "big [expletive] deal."

After Obama's reelection, the environment became a top priority

By Juliet Eilperin

On the night in early June 2008 when Barack Obama had finally won enough contests to secure the Democratic nomination for president, he marked the momentous occasion with a prediction.

"I am absolutely certain that generations from now, we will be able to look back and tell our children that this was the moment when we began to provide care for the sick and good jobs to the jobless; this was the moment when the rise of the oceans began to slow and our planet began to heal," he said at a campaign rally in St. Paul, Minn. on the last night of voting of that primary season. Obama had made history by winning the nomination, and that night he spoke from the same stage where John McCain, his GOP rival, would accept his party's nomination that September.

Obama's rhetoric about his impact on the Earth struck some as grandiose and fanciful. The line was mocked by critics, and by every scientific measure the planet's precarious situation has gotten worse, not better since he made that claim.

Each year of Obama's presidency so far has been among the top 10 hottest years on record. In 2015, the United States saw the most wildfires in recorded history. Atmospheric concentrations of carbon dioxide — the best measure of the global increase in heat-trapping gases — continue to rise. So do sea levels.

As these indicators worsened during the course of his first term, many environmentalists complained that Obama was too focused on the ailing economy and not sufficiently interested in passing legislation that would have imposed nationwide limits on greenhouse gas emissions. In fact, the president and some aides were laying the groundwork for these cuts — but played down their significance.

Several members of the president's inner circle were worried that pressing too hard on environmental issues in the midst of a deep recession could be politically costly. Although the Democratic-controlled House managed in the summer of 2009 to narrowly pass legislation that would have adopted a cap-and-trade system to help curb greenhouse gas emissions nationally, the bill stalled in the Senate as Democrats focused on passing the Affordable Care Act instead.

But Lisa Jackson, who headed the Environmental Protection Agency, pressed ahead with a series of public health and auto-efficiency rules that — coupled with broader energy market trends — helped cut greenhouse gas emissions significantly.

In 2009, the EPA reached a deal with the U.S. auto industry, which had just been bailed out by the federal government, to impose the first-ever carbon limits on cars and light trucks. The agency implemented a mercury and air toxic standard in 2011, which was 21 years in the making and required tighter pollution controls on many power plants. It also issued a Cross-State Air Pollution Rule, which further cut emissions, along with multiple regional haze rules.

At the very time that these federal rules were making coal-generated electricity more expensive, an explosion in hydraulic fracturing, an efficient technique for extracting natural gas, was making U.S. gas cheaper. And Obama's controversial stimulus package, the American Recovery and Reinvestment Act of 2009, kick-started clean energy and energy-efficiency projects across the country.

But the president and his aides played down the climate agenda, fearing that it would imperil his reelection. They adopted an "all of the above" approach to U.S. energy production.

They welcomed the expansion of natural gas drilling — much

Flames light up the landscape at a fracking operation near Tilden, Tex. (Michael S. Williamson/The Washington Post)

of which was happening on private land, either on the Great Plains or in states such as Pennsylvania — and appeared to be open to approving a massive pipeline to transport heavy crude oil from Canada's oil sands region to Gulf Coast refineries in Texas.

Many environmentalists were frustrated. "The administration didn't spend too much political capital on cutting carbon," said Sierra Club executive director Michael Brune.

Activists chained themselves to the White House fence to protest the Keystone XL pipeline, arguing that it was one of the few ways Obama could act unilaterally to combat the use of fossil fuels.

And act he did, once he was reelected. From the moment Obama won a second term, climate change and the environment became one of his top priorities. Surprising even some of his top aides, he declared in his second inaugural address: "We will respond to the threat of climate change, knowing that the failure to do so would betray our children and future generations." Within six months he had unveiled a climate action plan, and he pressed ahead on a range of issues, including mandatory carbon limits on existing power plants and negotiation of a major new global climate agreement in Paris. He also rejected the Keystone XL pipeline, arguing that allowing it to proceed would send the wrong message at a time when the United States was committed to tackling global warming, and he went to Alaska to draw America's attention to what a melting glacier looks like.

The president came to realize in his second term, Brune said, "that to win on climate you can't avoid a fight. He recognizes there are adversaries on the climate fight, and he has not missed an opportunity to take them on."

Obama's legacy on climate will depend on who follows him in the Oval Office. But already, these policies have helped transform the American landscape.

As of June 2016, 1 million U.S. homes boasted solar installations — a benchmark that took 40 years to reach. There are now more employees working in solar energy than in the coal industry, and two of the fastest-growing careers include wind-turbine technician and solar-panel installer.

At the same time, the coal industry continues to shrink. Coal accounted for nearly half of U.S. electricity generation when Obama took office; now, it amounts to a third.

"Just since 2011, when the president's power plant regulations began to bite, about 68,000 coal miners have lost their jobs — high-wage jobs that this administration has failed to replace, let alone create," said Luke Popovich, a spokesman for the National Mining Association.

His allies and critics rarely agree but on this they do: By the time he leaves office, Obama will have pushed through one of the most ambitious environmental agendas in U.S. history.

Guns, grief and gridlock: Time and time again, President Obama addressed a nation in mourning

The Obama post-mass-shooting official statement became a recurring feature of the past eight years. He cried for the children of Sandy Hook, sang for the dead in Charleston, and was repeatedly angry at Congress for not making it more difficult for criminals, suspected terrorists and mentally ill people to buy guns.

"Somehow this has become routine. The reporting has become routine. My response here, from this podium, has become routine," he lamented in the fall of 2015, after a student opened fire in an English class, killing nine at a community college in Oregon. After five police officers were killed in an ambush in Dallas in July, Obama acknowledged disappointment and failure in his ability to alter the terms of the gun debate.

"I'm not naive. I've spoken at too many memorials during the course of this presidency. I've hugged too many families that lost a loved one to senseless violence," he said. "I've seen how inadequate my own words have been. "

The following are the full remarks given by Obama in January 2016, shortly after he introduced new executive actions intended to curb gun violence. He became emotional as he delivered this speech, tearing up as he spoke to the nation.

Remarks by President Barack Obama
Time: 11:40 am EDT, Date: Tuesday, January 5th, 2016

OBAMA: Thank you.

Thank you, everybody.

Please have a seat.

Thank you so much.

Mark, I want to thank you for your introduction. I still remember the first time we met and the time we spent together, the conversation we had about Daniel.

And that changed me that day. And my hope earnestly has been that it would change the country.

Five years ago this week, a sitting member of Congress and 18 others were shot at at a supermarket in Tucson, Arizona. It wasn't the first time I had to talk to the nation in response to a mass shooting, nor would it be the last: Fort Hood, Binghamton, Aurora, Oak Creek, Newtown, the Navy Yard, Santa Barbara, Charleston, San Bernardino.OBAMA: Too many.

Thanks to a great medical team and the love of her husband, Mark, my dear friend and colleague Gabby Giffords survived. She's here with us today with her wonderful mom.

It was thanks to a great medical team, her wonderful husband, Mark, who by the way the last time I met with Mark -- this is just a small aside. You may know Mark's twin brother is in outer space.

He came to the office and I said how often are you talking to him. He says well I usually talk to him every day, but the call was coming in right before the meeting, so I think I may have not answered his call, which made me feel kind of bad.

That's a long-distance call.

So I told him if his brother Scott is calling today that he should take it. Just turn the ringer off.

I was there with Gabby when she was still in the hospital, and we didn't think necessarily at that point that she was going to survive. And that visit right before memorial, about an hour later, Gabby first opened her eyes. And I remember talking to her mom about that.

But I know the pain that she and her family have endured these past five years and the rehabilitation and the work and the effort to recover from shattering injuries. And then I think of all the American who aren't as fortunate. Every single year, more than

30,000 Americans have their lives cut short byguns -- 30,000. Suicides, domestic violence, gang shootouts, accidents.

Hundreds of thousands of Americans have lost brothers and sisters or buried their own children. Many have had to learn to live with a disability or learn to live without the love of their life. A number of those people are here today. They can tell you some stories. In this room right here, there are a lot of stories. There's a lot of heartache. There's a lot of resilience, there's a lot of strength, but there's also a lot of pain. And this is just a small sample.

The United States of America is not the only country on Earth with violent or dangerous people, we are not inherently more prone to violence. But we are the only advanced country on Earth that sees this kind of mass violence erupt with this kind of frequency. It doesn't happen in other advanced countries. It's not even close. OBAMA: And as I've said before, somehow we've become numb to it and we start thinking that this is normal. And instead of thinking about how to solve the problem, this has become one of our most polarized, partisan debates. Despite the fact that there's a general consensus in American about what needs to be done, and that's part of the reason why on Thursday, I'm going to hold a townhall meeting in Virginia on gun violence, because my goal here is to bring good people on both sides of this issue together for an open discussion.

I am not on the ballot again, I am not looking to score points. I think we can disagree without impugning other people's motives or without being disagreeable. We don't need to be talking past one another, but we do have to feel a sense of urgency about it.

In Dr. King's words, the fierce urgency of now, because people are dying. And the constant excuses for inaction no longer do, no longer suffice. That's why we are here today. Not to debate the last mass shooting, but to do something to prevent the next one.

To prove that the vast majority of Americans, even if our voices aren't always the loudest and most extreme, care enough about a little boy like Daniel to come together and take common-sense steps to save lives and protect more of our children.

Now, I want to be absolutely clear at the start. I have said this over and over again -- this also becomes routine. There is a ritual about this whole thing that I have to do. I believe in the Second Amendment. It is there, written on the paper, it guarantees a right to bear arms. No matter how many times people try to my words around, I taught constitutional law, I know a little bit about this.

I get it. But I also believe we can find ways to reduce gun violence consistent with the Second Amendment. I mean, think about it -- we all believe in the First Amendment, the guarantee of free speech. But we accept that you cannot yell "fire," in a theater. We understand there are some constraints on our freedom in order to protect innocent people.

We cherish our right to privacy, but we accept that you have to go through metal detectors before being allowed to board a plane. It's not because people like doing that, but we understand that is part of the price of living in a civilized society. And what's often ignored in this debate is that the majority of gun owners actually agree -- a majority of gun owners agree that we can respect the Second Amendment while keeping an irresponsible, lawbreaking feud from inflicting harm on a massive scale.

Today, background checks are required at gun stores. If a father wants to teach his daughter how to hunt, he can walk into a gun store, get a background check, purchase his weapon safely and responsibly. This is not seen as an infringement on the Second Amendment.

Contrary to the claims of what some gun rights' proponents have suggested, this has not been the first step in some slippery slope to mass confiscation. Contrary to claims of some presidential candidates, apparently before this meeting, this is not a plot to take away everybody's guns. You pass a background check, you purchase a firearm. OBAMA: The problem is, some gun sellers have been operating under a different set of rules. A violent felon can buy the exact same weapon over the Internet with no background check, no questions asked. A recent study found that about one in 30 people looking to buy guns on one website had criminal records. One out of 30 had a criminal record.

We're talking about individuals convicted of serious crimes -- aggravated assault, domestic violence, robbery, illegal gun possession; people with lengthy criminal histories buying deadly weapons all too easily. And this was just one website within the span of a few months.

So, we've created a system in which dangerous people are allowed to play by a different set of rules than a responsible gun owner who buys his or her gun the right way and subjects themselves to a background check. That doesn't make sense. Everybody should have to abide by the same rules. Most Americans and gun owners agree.

And that's what we tried to change three years ago after 26 Americans, including 20 children, were murdered at Sandy Hook Elementary. Two United States senators, Joe Manchin, a Democrat from West Virginia, and Pat Toomey, a Republican from Pennsylvania, both gun owners, both strong defenders of our Second Amendment rights, both with "A" grades from the NRA -- that's hard to get -- worked together in good faith, consulting with folks like our vice president, who's been a champion on this for a long time, to write a common sense compromise bill that would have required virtually everyone who buys a gun to get a background check. That was it -- pretty common sense stuff.

Ninety percent of Americans supported that idea. Ninety percent of Democrats in the Senate voted for that idea, but it failed because 90 percent of Republicans in the Senate voted against that idea.

How did this become such a partisan issue? Republican President George W. Bush once said, "I believe in background checks at gun shows or anywhere to make sure that guns don't get into the hands of people that shouldn't have them." Senator John McCain introduced a bipartisan measure to address the gun show loophole, saying, "We need this amendment because criminals and terrorists have exploited and are exploiting this very obvious loophole in our gun safety laws."

Even the NRA used to support expanded background checks. And by the way, most of its members still do. Most Republican voters still do. How did we get here? How did we get to the place where people think requiring a comprehensive background check means taking away people's guns?

Each time this comes up, we are fed the excuse that common sense reforms like background checks might not have stopped the last massacre or the one before that or the one before that. So, why bother trying? I reject that thinking.

We know we can't stop every act of violence, every act of evil in the world. But maybe we could try to stop one act of evil, one act of violence. Some of you may recall at the same time that Sandy Hook happened, a disturbed person in China took a knife and tried to kill with a knife a bunch of children in China, but most of them survived because he didn't have access to a powerful weapon. OBAMA: We maybe can't save everybody, but we could save some. Just as we don't prevent all traffic accidents, but we take steps to try to reduce traffic accidents. As Ronald Reagan once said, "If mandatory background checks could save more lives, it would be well worth making it the law of the land."

The bill before Congress three years ago met that test. Unfortunately too many senators failed theirs.

In fact, we know that background checks make a difference. After Connecticut passed a law requiring background checks and gun safety courses, gun deaths decreased by 40 percent. Forty percent.

Meanwhile, since Missouri repealed a law requiring comprehensive background checks and purchase permits, gun deaths have increased to an almost 50 percent higher than the national average. One study found, unsurprisingly, that criminals in Missouri now have easier access to guns.

And the evidence tells us that in states that require background checks, law-abiding Americans don't find it any harder to purchase guns whatsoever. Their guns have not been confiscated, their rights have not been infringed. And that's just the information we have access to.

With more research we could further improve gun safety just as with more research we've reduced traffic fatalities enormously over the last 30 years. We do research when cars, food, medicine, even toys harm people so that we make them safer. And you know what, research, science, those are good things. They work.

They do. But think about this. When it comes to an inherently deadly weapon, nobody argues thatguns are potentially deadly. Weapons that kill tens of thousands of Americans every year, Congress actually voted to make it harder for public health experts to conduct research into gun violence, Made it harder to collect data and facts and develop strategies to reduce gun violence. Even after San Bernardino, they refused to make it harder for terror suspects, who can't get on a plane, to buy semiautomatic weapons. That's not right.

That can't be right. So the gun lobby may be holding Congress hostage right now but they can't hold America hostage.

We do not have to accept that carnage is the price of freedom.

Now, I want to be clear, Congress still needs to act. The folks in this room will not rest until Congress does.

Because once Congress gets on board with common sense gun safety measures, we can reduce gun violence a whole lot more. But we also can't wait. Until we have a Congress that's in line with the majority of Americans, there are actions within my legal authority that we can take to help reduce gun violence and save more lives, actions that protect our rights and our kids.

After Sandy Hook, Joe and I worked together with our teams and we put forward a whole series of executive actions to try to tighten up the existing rules and systems that we had in place. But today we want to take it a step further. So let me outline what we're going to be doing.OBAMA: Number one, anybody in the business of selling firearms must get a license and conduct background checks or be subject to criminal prosecutions.

It doesn't matter whether you're doing it over the Internet or the gun show, it's not where you do it but what you do. We're also expanding background checks to cover violent criminals who try to buy some of the most dangerous firearms by hiding behind trusts and corporations and various cutouts.

We're also taking steps to make the background check system more efficient. Under the guidance of Jim Comey and the FBI and our Deputy Director Tom Brandon at ATF, we're going to hire more folks to process applications faster and we're going to bring an outdated background check system into the 21st century.

And these steps will actually lead to a smoother process for law- abiding gun owners, a smoother process for responsible gun dealers, a stronger process for protecting the people from -- the public from dangerous people. So that's number one.

Number two, we're going to do everything we can to ensure the smart and effective enforcement of gun safety laws that are already on the books, which means we're going to add 200 more ATF agents and investigators. We're going to require firearms dealers to report more or lost -- more lost or stolenguns on a timely basis. We're working with advocates to protect victims of domestic abuse from gun violence where too often...

Where too often people are not getting the protection they need.

Number three, we're going to do more to help those suffering from mental illness get the help that they need.

So high-profile mass shootings tend to shine a light on those few mentally unstable people who inflict harm on others, but the truth is that nearly two in three gun deaths are from suicides. So a lot of our work is to prevent people from hurting themselves. That's why we made sure that the Affordable Care Act, also known as Obamacare...

Finally...

Under that law, made sure that treatment for mental health was covered the same as treatment for any other illness. That's why we're going to invest $500 million to expand access to treatment across the country.

It's also why we're going to ensure that federal mental health records are submitted to the background check system and remove barriers that prevent states from reporting relevant information. If we can continue to destigmatize mental health issues, get folks proper care and fill gaps in the background check system, then we can spare more families the pain of losing a loved one to suicide.

And for those in Congress who so often rush to blame mental illness for mass shootings as a way of avoiding action on guns, here's your chance to support these efforts. Put your money where your mouth is.

Number four, we're going to boost gun safety technology. Today, many gun injuries and deaths are the result of legal guns that were stolen or misused or discharged accidentally. In 2013 alone, more than 500 people lost their lives to gun accidents and that includes 30 children younger than five years old.

In the greatest, most technologically advanced nation on Earth, there is no reason for this. We need to develop new technologies that make guns safer. If we can set it up so you can't unlock your phone unless you've got the right fingerprint, why can't we do the same thing for our guns?(APPLAUSE)

OBAMA: If there's an app that can help us find a missing tablet -- which happens to me often...

... the older I get.

If we can do it for your iPad, there's no reason we can't do it with a stolen gun. If a child can't open a bottle of aspirin, we should make sure they can't pull a trigger on a gun.

All right? So, we're going to advance research, we're going to work with the private sector to update firearms technology. And some gun retailers are already stepping up by refusing to finalize a purchase without a complete background check, or by refraining from selling semi-automatic weapons or high capacity magazines.

And I hope that more retailers and more manufacturers join

them, because they should care as much as anybody about a product that now kills almost as many Americans as car accidents.

I make this point because none of us can do this alone. I think Mark made that point earlier. All of us should be able to work together to find a balance that declares the rest of our rights are also important. Second Amendment rights are important, but there are other rights that we care about as well. And we have to be able to balance them, because our right to worship freely and safely -- that right was denied to Christians in Charleston, South Carolina.

And that was denied Jews in Kansas city, and that was denied Muslims in Chapel Hill and Sikhs in Oak Creek. They had rights too.

Our right to peaceful assembly, that right was robbed from moviegoers in Aurora and Lafayette. Our inalienable right to life, and liberty and the pursuit of happiness, those rights were stripped from college kids in Blacksburg and Santa Barbara, and from high-schoolers in Columbine, and from first graders in Newtown.

First graders. And from every family who never imagined that their loved one would be taken from our lives by a bullet from a gun.

Every time I think about those kids, it gets me mad. And by the way, it happens on the streets of Chicago every day.

So, all of us need to demand that Congress be brave enough to stand up to the gun lobby's lies. All of us need to stand up and protect its citizens. All of us need to demand governors, and legislators and businesses do their part to make our communities safer.

We need the wide majority of responsible gun owners, who grieve with us every time this happens and feel like your views are not being properly represented, to join with us to demand something better.

And we need voters who want safer gun laws, and who are disappointed in leaders who stand in their way to remember come election time.

I mean, some of this is just simple math. Yes, the gun lobby is loud and it is organized in defense of making it effortless for guns to be available for anybody, anytime.OBAMA: Well, you know what? The rest of us, we all have to be just as passionate. We have to be just as organized in the defense of our kids. This is not that complicated. The reason Congress blocks laws is because they want to win elections. If you make it hard for them to win an election if they block those laws, they'll change course, I promise.

And yes, it will be hard and it won't happen overnight. It won't happen during this Congress, it won't happen during my presidency. But a lot of things don't happen overnight. A woman's right to vote didn't happen overnight, the liberation of African-Americans didn't happen overnight. LGBT rights, that was decades worth of work. So just because it's hard that's no excuse not to try.

And if you have any doubt as to why you should feel that fierce urgency of now, think about what happened three weeks ago. Zavion Dobson was a sophomore at Fulton High School in Knoxville, Tennessee. He played football, beloved by his classmates and his teachers. His own mayor called him one of their city's success stories.

The week before Christmas, he headed to a friend's house to play video games. He wasn't in the wrong place at the wrong time, he hadn't made a bad decision. He was exactly where any other kid would be -- your kid, my kids. And then gunmen started firing, and Zavion, who was in high school -- hadn't even gotten started in life -- dove on top of three girls to shield them from the bullets, and he was shot in the head and the girls were spared. He gave his life to save theirs. An act of heroism a lot bigger than anything we should ever expect from a 15-year-old. Greater love hath no man than this than a man lay down his life for his friends.

We are not asked to do what Zavion Dobson did, we're not asked to have shoulders that big, a heart that strong, reactions that quick. I'm not asking people to have that same level of courage or sacrifice or love, but if we love our kids and care about their prospects and if we love this country and care about its future, then we can find the courage to vote, we can find the courage to get mobilized and organized, we can find the courage to cut through all the noise and do what a sensible country would do.

That's what we're doing today, and tomorrow, we should do more and we should do more the day after that. And if we do, we'll leave behind a nation that's stronger than the one we inherited and worthy of the sacrifice of a young man life Zavion. Thank you very much, everybody. God bless you. Thank you.

CHAPTER 5

OBAMA AND THE WORLD

Obama's foreign policy of restraint was both pragmatic and problematic

By Ivo H. Daalder

Barack Obama came to office believing his predecessor had over-reached in the world, notably in his conduct of the global war on terrorism. Convinced that the United States had become overextended and stood more alone on the world stage than ever before, Obama had run on a platform of ending the wars in Iraq and Afghanistan and regaining the trust of the world. Facing the most significant financial crisis in generations, he stressed the importance of sharing more of the burdens and responsibilities of global leadership with others.

The result was a foreign policy that minimized reliance on large-scale military action and maximized cooperation with others. Obama steadily reduced the U.S. military commitment to Iraq and, following a brief surge in military activity, transformed the U.S. presence in Afghanistan into a small training mission. He sharply increased the use of small, targeted military operations, but he steadfastly refused to get drawn into another major engagement of the kind launched by his predecessors — whether in Syria, Libya, Ukraine or elsewhere.

Instead, Obama reached out to other nations, convinced that meeting new threats, as he said in his first inaugural address, demanded "greater effort, even greater cooperation and understanding between nations." Even to America's enemies, Obama offered to extend a hand to those willing to receive it.

This more restrained policy was broadly welcomed by U.S.

President Obama shakes hands with troops after delivering remarks at Fort Bragg, N.C., on Dec. 14, 2011. (Jim Watson/Agence France-Presse via Getty Images)

allies and friends abroad. Favorable views of America's role in the world rose sharply, and generally remained there for the duration of his presidency.

The positive reviews were hardly universal. Critics at home and abroad blame his minimalist approach to military engagement for many of the ills in the world today. To them, Obama's restraint led to a world in which Syria has become a humanitarian nightmare, a source of destabilizing refugee flows into the Middle East and Europe and an incubator of the Islamic State. They blame him for allowing a world in which Vladimir Putin has returned as a Russian strongman, invading neighbors and flexing his military muscle in the Middle East and beyond; and where China has risen as a geostrategic adversary in the Asia-Pacific region. As Donald Trump put it, the Obama legacy abroad is "death, destruction, terrorism and weakness."

The critics have a point. While saying he would never take options off the table, Obama made clear that restraint was his primary choice. The result has been that those who wish America ill may have had little incentive not to defy it. Exhibit number one for these critics was the President's failure to enforce his own red line in Syria--a failure that contributed to a perception of weakness.

Obama is right to note that working with Moscow to get rid of Syrian chemical weapons was an outcome no amount of bombing could have accomplished on its own. But he is wrong to dismiss the idea that a president's words matter, especially in foreign affairs. When other nations come to doubt those words, they may hedge their bets in working with Washington, and our ability to get them to align with us against common foes or in pursuit of common purposes will be lessened.

Yet it is simplistic to assign blame for all the world's ills to Obama's more restrained policies abroad. It is far from clear — nor have his critics demonstrated — that a more aggressive policy would have resulted in better outcomes. And as the decade preceding his presidency showed, the opposite may well have been true. At the same time, the assumption that everything in the world — for good or ill — happens because of American action or inaction greatly overstates our power and influence.

The situations in Syria, Iraq and Libya, and the rise of the Islamic State and terror networks, have far more to do with the long-standing crisis of governance in the Arab world than with how much force America is willing to use. Similarly, Putin had his own reasons for invading Ukraine and intervening in Syria — above all, to bolster his standing at home and defend Moscow's interests in both countries. And whether we like it or not, China is a rising great power and will increasingly act like great powers do, seeking to extend their sphere of influence regionally and globally.

The challenge for U.S. foreign policy is not to deny these realities, but to forge policies that protect and enhance America's interests in ways that take them into account. Indeed, this world of diffused power and increased global threats requires a different kind of American leadership — a 21st-century form of leadership.

That is the kind in which Obama believes, and which he largely exercised. To Obama, not every global problem has an American solution. Although few such problems can be solved without America's direct involvement, in most instances it requires the active participation of others to succeed. Effective leadership in today's world isn't just about who is in the driver's seat, but about who comes along for the ride. More often than not, it requires sharing — of responsibilities, of burdens and of credit. It also requires a willingness to compromise to gain consensus. And while military force has a role to play, it is not the only or even the most decisive instrument available to the United States in today's complex world.

"The time has come to realize that the old habits, the old arguments, are irrelevant to the challenges faced by our people," Obama told the U.N. General Assembly in his first annual address there. "Together, we must build new coalitions that bridge old divides." America seeks "a future of peace and prosperity," but this can be achieved only "if we recognize that all nations have rights, but all nations have responsibilities as well. That is the bargain that makes this work. That must be the guiding principle of international cooperation."

Perhaps nowhere was Obama's view of U.S. leadership more evident than with respect to the Iranian nuclear threat. From the outset, he made clear that he sought to engage Tehran to end its nuclear weapons program. Although he did keep the option of force on the table, Obama preferred a negotiated deal, which he believed would be more lasting and less costly. To achieve it, he forged a global coalition--backed by the U.N. Security Council and all its permanent members--that imposed punishing sanctions on Iran. Once negotiations were underway, the involvement of all the key players effectively limited Tehran's options.

The result was a deal that capped Iran's nuclear ambitions for a decade or more and put in place the most intrusive inspection regime ever negotiated.

Addressing the growing threat of climate change offered another opportunity to display this more inclusive type of leadership. For years, the biggest obstacle to an international agreement cutting greenhouse gas emissions had been the unwillingness of developing countries to commit to such reductions. Obama realized that in this, China was key, and so he worked to gain Beijing's agreement to cut its emissions. That bilateral agreement, announced

Soldiers based at Fort Stewart, Ga., sit in the belly of a C-17 aircraft at Sather Air Base in Baghdad on Nov. 30, 2010, as they begin their journey home after a year in Iraq. (Maya Alleruzzo/Associated Press)

in November 2014, provided the foundation for the successful conclusion of the 2015 Paris negotiations, in which all nations pledged to cut emissions to slow the rise in global temperatures.

Cooperative leadership also was Obama's goal in more traditional settings, including Europe and Asia. Even before Russian actions in Ukraine necessitated collective action, strengthening NATO was an important concern of the administration. All U.S. troops in Afghanistan were placed under NATO command, missile defense deployments were transitioned from a system focused on defending the United States from Europe to a NATO system defending NATO in Europe, and a new strategic concept was put in place to guide the alliance in this new world. Following the Russian invasion of Ukraine, Washington worked with its partners in the European Union to put significant sanctions on Moscow, and with its NATO allies to bolster the defense of Eastern Europe.

Obama indicated early on that the weight of U.S. foreign policy effort and attention would shift to Asia, the most dynamic and economically most important region of the world. One immediate effect of the "Asia pivot" was to provide allies and friends a counterbalance to a rising China, many of whom in previous years had begun to slide into Beijing's orbit. Stronger alliances with Japan, South Korea, the Philippines and Australia were matched by improved relations with Indonesia, Vietnam and other Southeast Asian nations. And through the negotiation of the Trans-Pacific Partnership trade agreement, Obama was able to bring together the most critical U.S. partners in the Asia-Pacific region, including key partners in North and South America, in a major pact that, once approved, will set the rules for trade for years to come.

A foreign policy of restraint was inevitable, given the strong disinclination of the American public to pursue more military adventures, and the severe financial crisis undermining the economy. One can argue the extent of such moderation, but not the need for it.

Obama surely made his share of mistakes, including misreading the Arab Spring. He believed that support for the ouster of authoritarian regimes put America and his administration on the right side of history. But calling for the overthrow of dictators while doing little--in some cases, nothing--to help those who sought their downfall was a contradiction that has already had significant, long-term costs.

The need to balance power remains a central factor in global politics. Obama played down, and perhaps even underestimated, the geopolitical challenge posed by Russia and China, and the importance of signaling resolve in the face of clear provocations. And he never really invested in the personal relationships abroad or at home that might have helped forge more agreement on the direction and requirements of America's relations with the world.

But with all its flaws, the course Obama chose abroad was arguably a realistic one for turbulent times and a new century. More than his predecessors--and his critics--he understood the complexities of our world and of power and leadership. A new American president, crafting an approach to a world in turmoil, could do worse than to take a page out of the Obama playbook.

Ivo Daalder is president of the Chicago Council on Global Affairs. He served as U.S. ambassador to NATO from 2009 to 2013.

Although much of the world still views Obama favorably, the dominant emotion in the Middle East is disappointment

By Kevin Sullivan

When President Obama strode to the podium at Cairo University on June 4, 2009, he faced a Muslim world bursting with optimism about his middle name — Hussein! — along with his barrier-bashing skin color, and a heart they believed was wide open to their concerns and dreams.

"Assalaamu alaykum," Obama said, using the traditional Arabic salutation Muslims use to greet one another. "Peace be upon you."

He called for "a new beginning between the United States" and the world's billion Muslims. He promised to close the reviled prison at Guantanamo Bay, to "personally pursue" Palestinian-Israeli peace and to bring U.S. troops home from Iraq. Obama said he would invest billions in Afghanistan and Pakistan; seek a nuclear deal with Iran; encourage deeper ties in science, education and business; and promote women's rights.

"It's easier to start wars than to end them," he said to applause. "It's easier to blame others than to look inward. It's easier to see what is different about someone than to find the things we share. But we should choose the right path, not just the easy path. ... We have the power to make the world we seek, but only if we have the courage to make a new beginning."

"Barack Obama, we love you," shouted someone in the audience.

More than seven years later, the romance has withered. Along with some lingering fondness, there are feelings of bitterness and regret, and nagging questions about what might have been.

"They will remember him as the first black president; someone like Muhammad Ali. But not like Martin Luther King Jr.," said Hisham Kassem, former publisher of Al-Masry Al-Youm, Egypt's only independent newspaper.

> *"You can't hold Obama responsible for what happened in Egypt. Egyptians do determine their fate. . . . [But] Obama has disappointed people more, and that's what his legacy is. . . . His pledges were for the people to be treated as real human beings with rights and [to] help propel democracy. But if you are still doing deals with corrupt dictators, how does that fulfill your promises?"*
>
> *Wael Eskandar, activist, Egypt*

Although much of the world still views Obama favorably, the dominant emotion in the Middle East is disappointment. Just under half of those in Israel and Turkey have confidence in him, according to a 40-nation Pew Research Center survey conducted in June 2015. Few expressed favorable views of the U.S. president: about a third of Lebanese, 15 percent of Palestinians and 14 percent of Jordanians.

Saleh Mohammed Saleh, an Afghan legislator from Kunar province, said he and other Afghans were encouraged when Obama reached out just months after his first inauguration. But during the years of Obama's presidency, Saleh said, both the world and the region had become more unstable. "He claimed credit for killing [Osama] bin Laden and some Taliban leaders, but are we safer than before? Are the world and the U.S. safer? I don't think so at all. The region is on fire."

The reasons Muslims give for their disillusionment are almost too many to count: seven years of drone strikes, deepening chaos in Iraq and the rise of the Islamic State, continued violence in Afghanistan, the collapse of Libya, the lack of Israeli-Palestinian

Protesters light fireworks in Cairo to celebrate President Hosni Mubarak's resignation on Feb. 11, 2011. (Linda Davidson/The Washington Post)

Two Syrian rebels take sniper positions in central Aleppo on Oct. 18, 2012. (Javier Manzano/Agence France-Presse via Getty Images)

A protester wearing a Tunisian flag makes his way past closed shops toward sporadic gunfire in Tunis, Tunisia, in February 2011. (Nikki Kahn/The Washington Post)

progress, ongoing U.S. support for autocratic governments, the failure to close Guantanamo.

> *"I think it was the right decision in terms of protecting the Libyan civilians. But the follow-up after that decision, leaving Libya alone after the fall of the regime, that was the tragic mistake. . . . You let Libya become a hub for terrorists."*
> *Mahmoud Jibril, former opposition leader, Libya*

Some see the Iran nuclear deal — something the administration considers a signature foreign policy achievement — as a positive step to keep the ayatollahs in Tehran from getting a nuclear weapon. "The idea of minimizing the risk of a nuclear Iran or multilateral intervention against Iran is definitely a plus for the Middle East," said Amr Adly, a political analyst and researcher with the Carnegie Middle East Center.

But critics in the region — echoing naysayers at home — call the agreement a naïve capitulation that does the opposite, arguing that it simply allows Iran to postpone its nuclear ambitions in exchange for renewed stature in the world and a windfall of billions of dollars that it will use to spread its state-sponsored terror.

Hisham Melhem, Washington bureau chief of Saudi Arabia–owned al-Arabiya News Channel, said that he applauded the deal but that Obama should have used the negotiations to pressure Iran on other fronts.

"He was silent on human rights in Iran," Melhem said. "He did not check, or try to check, Iran's proxy wars in Iraq and Syria."

> *"In the first term of Obama, Iraq wasn't among his priorities. . . . We hope the next American administration will be more serious in supporting Iraq, because now Iraq needs all the support it can get."*
> *Ibrahim Bahr al-Ulloum, parliamentarian, Iraq*

And then there is Syria, the Rubik's Cube of a civil war that has left hundreds of thousands dead and more than half the population displaced from their homes or scattered as refugees abroad. In

Lebanon, Turkey and Jordan, it has created a humanitarian nightmare. In Europe, the flow of more than a million fleeing migrants has led to right-wing nationalism with ominous historical echoes.

Obama has defended his early decision to limit support to rebels fighting President Bashar al-Assad, and the quick erasure of a "red line" drawn over Assad's use of chemical weapons, as wise restraint. But to many in the region, his actions seemed like dithering.

"Obama allowed human rights violations committed by the Syrian regime to happen every day," said Melhem Riachi, an analyst who teaches communications at Lebanon's Holy Spirit University of Kaslik. "This do-nothing policy actually empowered terrorism by aiding the rise of extremist Muslim groups," he said, and "actually strengthened the [Assad] regime."

The resulting vacuum in Syria itself allowed the Islamic State to grow from its Iraqi roots. As it has spread its medieval horrors across the region, it has displaced al-Qaeda as the source of inspiration for ultra-violent militants who have struck brutally from Istanbul to Paris to San Bernardino.

Some of the things Obama promised to do, such as the closure of Guantanamo, were blocked by a recalcitrant Congress. He did bring the troops home from Iraq, and billions have been spent in Afghanistan. Yet both those countries remain at war. And despite years of effort, there has been no substantive improvement to the Israeli-Palestinian struggle.

> *"I think it is very clear as far as the Palestinians are concerned, the Obama administration has been a huge disappointment."*
>
> George Giacaman, university professor,
> Palestinian territories

The Arab Spring, which brought hope to millions in the Middle East as well as to the Obama administration, limps on in Tunisia, where it began. But it lies in ruins in Egypt, Libya, Yemen, Syria and beyond.

Laying the region's manifold problems at Obama's doorstep grossly oversimplifies some of the world's most complex and confounding dynamics. And the complaints follow a familiar historical pattern: high expectations that the United States can solve a problem, followed by inevitable disappointment when it cannot. Too much intervention. Not enough. Too much emphasis on democracy and human rights. Too little.

"You have this element of association with the Obama administration and anarchy in the region," said Adly, the Carnegie researcher. "So he's not that popular at all nowadays. ... You have this mainstream distrust in whatever the U.S. does, and a gross overestimation for what the U.S. can do. ... There is definitely a disenchantment with Obama."

Embers of hope still glow in the hearts of some: Said Ghorayeb, a writer who lives in Beirut, is one of those who still see Obama as the world leader most capable and inclined to ease Muslim suffering.

> *"President Obama brought only negative changes to Afghanistan. A majority of youths are unemployed, security is bad and every day we hear of attacks. The money sent ... under his presidency went to corrupt government officials, not ordinary people."*
>
> *Ezmarai Nesari, taxi driver, Afghanistan*

"Our country has been burdened so much," Ghorayeb said of Lebanon. "These refugees — this situation — is a ticking time bomb, and God only knows when it will explode and destroy what is left of one of the few free and democratic countries in the region."

But Melhem of al-Arabiya said Obama too often is more words than actions. "He's an honorable man. He's an extremely gifted and smart man. But he's not really a fighter."

"He went to Cairo and he introduced himself to a billion-plus Muslims in the world through a speech. He gives all these difficult speeches on terrorism, on drones, on race, on all of these issues, and they are beautifully crafted," Melham said. "But you get the impression that he thinks his words are a substitute for actions."

With reporting from Loveday Morris in Baghdad; Sudarsan Raghavan in Cairo; Hugh Naylor and Suzan Haidamous in Beirut; Pam Constable, Mohammad Sharif and Sayed Salahuddin in Kabul; and Ruth Eglash in Jerusalem.

A renewed relationship with Cuba was one of the administration's signature achievements

By Karen DeYoung

On the day that President Obama was to arrive in Cuba in March 2016, Alberto Moreno stood outside his open front door in the unreconstructed part of Old Havana, a neighborhood where crumbling, faded buildings abut narrow streets, and the thick, hot air smells of dust, sweat and cooking.

"People always think Cuba is the worst country in the world," said Moreno, a 30-something cook at a local brewery. "They think they're going to see military people with rifles everywhere. But look around," he said, motioning at the Sunday morning scene of chatting neighbors and sleepy pedicab drivers waiting for customers.

What Obama was going to experience in Cuba, Moreno asserted with no small amount of national pride, was "tranquility and calm," and people jostling for a look at him and shouting, "Obama, Obama, Obama, just like it is in every other country" he visits.

And so it was. During Obama's 2 1/2-day trip to the Cuban capital, those Habaneros, as residents of Havana call themselves, who crossed paths with the president ogled and shouted, while the rest went about their business.

But few Cubans were oblivious to the history being made. In the space of 15 short months, from the first announcement of normalization in December 2014 to the presidential visit, the official hostility that had defined U.S.-Cuba relations for more than half a century was over. Diplomatic relations were reestablished, nascent

President Obama, Michelle Obama and the first lady's mother, Marian Robinson, take a tour through Old Havana on March 20, 2016. (Pablo Martinez Monsivais/Associated Press)

business ties were forged, and regularly scheduled American planes full of American visitors were about to descend.

In meetings with Cuban entrepreneurs and students, and a news conference and speech broadcast live on national television, the U.S. president smiled broadly and spoke of freedom and friendship, presenting a stark and vibrant contrast to Cuba's dour communist leaders.

As Obama prepared to leave office, it was clear that the long-term objectives he set for the opening would not be achieved during his presidency. Although there has been some minor movement, state control over Cuban political life and over most aspects of the economy remains firmly in place. Arrests continue for dissent and free expression.

Still, the building of a diplomatic bridge across the 90 miles of open sea between Florida and the Cuban shore was a signature achievement, at least one successful item on Obama's original presidential bucket list that no future administration is likely to reverse.

Although Obama has used his executive powers to ease trade,

President Obama and Cuban President Raúl Castro attend an exhibition baseball game between the Cuban national team and the Tampa Bay Rays in Havana on March 22, 2016. (Chip Somodevilla/Getty Images)

travel and other restrictions, only Congress can remove the remaining embargo and U.S. travel limits on Cuba. Bills calling for both have steadily gained sponsors.

But "the fact of the matter is that the American people and the Cuban people overwhelmingly want this to happen," Ben Rhodes, Obama's deputy national security adviser, said last summer. "Frankly, whatever the political realities in either country, for somebody to try to turn this off, they would have to be working against the overwhelming desires of their own people.

"That ship has sailed," Rhodes said.

When Obama first proposed talking to the leaders of America's most ardent adversaries, during a Democratic primary debate in 2007, he shocked Republicans and Democrats. "The notion that somehow not talking to countries is punishment to them ... is ridiculous," he replied when asked whether he was willing to meet with rulers of places such as Iran, North Korea and Cuba. Presidents of both parties, he pointed out, had maintained dialogue with the Soviet Union during the darkest days of the Cold War.

His comments caused "one of the first big hubbubs in my Presidential campaign" and sent shivers down the spines of aides who feared he would lose the important Cuban-American vote in Florida, Obama recalled in a recent interview with the New Yorker.

But his theory, Obama said, was that "Cuba is a tiny, poor country that poses no genuine threat to the United States." At the same time, in terms of promoting change on the island, "in this era of the Internet and global capital movements ... openness is a more powerful change agent than isolation." Finally, Obama said he concluded, "if you are interested in promoting freedom, independence, civic space inside of Cuba," things such as allowing money to be sent to Cubans would allow more individuals the wherewithal to build a future apart from government control.

Obama won Florida in the 2008 election and quickly used his presidential authority to lift restrictions on remittances and Cuban American travel to the island. Over the next several years, the administration chipped away at the embargo. But it was not until after he was elected to a second term that Obama set his sights on normalizing relations and assigned Rhodes to open secret negotiations with a willing government in Havana.

The Cuba dialogue went far more smoothly than concurrent negotiations with Iran over its nuclear program. The Iran talks, during years of publicly announced meetings, were multilateral — with the administration having to deal not only with a recalcitrant Tehran but with its own negotiating partners, including Russia, China and European powers.

And because no one knew they were taking place — even the State Department was kept in the dark until nearly the end — negotiations with Cuba were shielded from the domestic political pressures that could have derailed them.

It turned out to be one of the administration's best-kept secrets. Public announcements by Obama and Cuban President Raúl Castro on Dec. 17, 2014, astounded both nations. Although some in Congress denounced it as a capitulation to the repressive Cuban government, most appeared to agree with Obama's observation that decades of antagonism had changed nothing on the island and that it was time to give a new policy a chance.

"Like so many people in both of our countries," he said in his televised speech in Havana on March 22, 2016, "my lifetime has spanned a time of isolation between us. The Cuban Revolution took place the same year that my father came to the United States from Kenya. The Bay of Pigs took place the year that I was born. The next year, the entire world held its breath, watching our two countries, as humanity came as close as we ever have to the horror of nuclear war.

"As the decades rolled by, our governments settled into a seemingly endless confrontation, fighting battles through proxies. In a world that remade itself time and again, one constant was the conflict between the United States and Cuba."

Differences remained, Obama cautioned, and the two countries continued to be divided on their systems of government, their economic models and their ideas about individual rights.

But "I have come here to bury the last remnant of the Cold War in the Americas," he said. "I have come here to extend the hand of friendship to the Cuban people."

Despite hopes of a strong partnership between the U.S. and China, a rocky relationship persisted

By John Pomfret

In April 2009, a few months after he took office, President Obama scheduled a summit in Beijing with then-Chinese president Hu Jintao. The Obama administration was faced with a decision. The Dalai Lama was planning to visit Washington and wanted to meet the president. From George H.W. Bush on, no president had denied the exiled Tibetan leader an audience. Hoping to make a good impression on his soon-to-be Chinese hosts, however, Obama decided to postpone the meeting until after he had seen Hu.

Obama was the first president in decades to enter the White House without having criticized the China policy of its previous occupant. Focused on the global war on terror, President George W. Bush had shelved his earlier idea that China was a "strategic competitor" and had maintained good ties with Beijing.

Obama's team was eager to build on Bush's successes. What better way to show America's sincerity, the White House figured, than starting off with a concession? But what began as a relationship infused with the hope that the United States and China would partner to confront global problems ended up as an even more competitive face-off between the two Pacific powers.

Obama administration officials had given China other indications that the president wanted to be China's partner, even its friend. Traveling to Beijing in February 2009, Secretary of State Hillary Clinton signaled that the administration would not let its

President Obama walks with Chinese President Hu Jintao at Diaoyutai
State Guesthouse in Beijing on Nov. 16, 2009. (Pete Souza/White House
via Getty Images)

traditional support of human rights "interfere with the global economic crisis, the global climate change crisis and the security crisis."
And in the first China-related speech from the administration,
Deputy Secretary of State James Steinberg made an unprecedented
public call for "a core, if tacit, bargain" between the two powers.

Washington needed to show China that it welcomed China's
rise, he said on Oct. 5, 2009. In exchange, China should assure
America that its rise "will not come at the expense of the security
and well-being of others." Steinberg called for "strategic reassurance" on both sides of the Pacific.

The Chinese saw the olive branches as a sign of weakness.
"Strategic Reassurance? Yes, Please!" went the headline in the
People's Daily. The United States should reassure China, it said,
by ending all arms sales to Taiwan and all military surveillance
activities off China's coast.

Then, just weeks later, Obama was subject to the shabbiest
treatment of any American president visiting China ever; his
remarks were censored during a question-and-answer session with

President Obama greets the audience after a town hall meeting at the Shanghai Science and Technology Museum on Nov. 16, 2009. (Saul Loeb/Agence France-Presse via Getty Images)

A May 11, 2015, aerial photo purportedly shows Chinese vessels at Mischief Reef in the South China Sea's Spratly Islands. (Pool photo by Ritchie B. Tongo/Getty)

A large portrait of former North Korean leader Kim Il Sung is surrounded by thousands in a torch parade in Pyongyang on May 10, 2016. (Linda Davidson/The Washington Post)

students in Shanghai. Whereas a previous Chinese president, Jiang Zemin, had engaged in a wide-ranging joint news conference with a visiting President Bill Clinton in 1998, Hu did not answer a single question with Obama when the two met the press. The public encounter was so frosty that it was parodied on "Saturday Night Live." At home, some in the media portrayed Obama as a deadbeat debtor kowtowing to America's banker, the Chinese Communist Party.

Obama's bumpy summit in China coupled with China's increasingly aggressive claims to all of the South China Sea and to islands administered by Japan laid the foundation for a change in the president's attitude toward China and a transformation of U.S. policy toward Asia. Ever since Richard Nixon went to China in 1972, American presidents had viewed China as the sun around which U.S. relations with all of Asia revolved. When he went to China in 1998, President Bill Clinton famously bypassed Japan, a sign that from Washington's perspective Tokyo played second fiddle to Beijing.

But China's failure to evolve disappointed many who had been hopeful about the partnership. They were distressed that there was still no free market economy and about the continued crackdowns on dissent and the moves to limit the reach of Western business in China. In addition, China's unrelenting cyberespionage and pilfering of American industrial secrets outraged many in the U.S. government, including the president. Obama was the first American president to go public with his exasperation, dubbing China a "free rider" in a global system built by the United States. In an August 2014 interview with the New York Times, the president noted that China's unwillingness to shoulder responsibility had allowed it "to secure the benefits of the global trading system with none of the responsibilities." Obama coined an expression "to do a Hu Jintao," poking fun at the Chinese president's habit of monotonously reciting his talking points.

Starting in 2010, the Obama administration began to put more emphasis on its alliances in Asia than on its hopes for a breakthrough with Beijing. To be sure, Obama continued to push China to maintain sanctions on Iran, which ultimately led to a deal to delay Iran's ability to build a nuclear bomb. He also reached an understanding with President Xi Jinping, Hu Jintao's successor, to control greenhouse gases, setting the stage for the Paris Agreement on climate change.

But in most of Asia, the Obama administration focused on shoring up relations with the Asian nations around China. It drew closer to Japan and South Korea. It gave vocal support to members of the Association of Southeast Asian Nations, worried about China's claims to the South China Sea.

It was Hillary Clinton, Obama's first secretary of state, who led the policy change, calling it, in an October 2011 essay in Foreign Policy magazine, a "pivot" toward Asia. Although much of the media attention on the pivot focused on America's enhanced security commitments to the region, trade played an equally important role.

Americans first came to the Pacific in the 18th century as merchants, and in the 21st century the Asia Pacific was poised to lead global growth. In November 2015, Obama administration officials pulled together the largest free-trade deal in U.S. history, the Trans-Pacific Partnership, linking 12 countries on the Pacific. China was not on the list.

But, significantly, the TPP has not gotten the congressional approval it needs, and Clinton, an architect of the trade deal while she was secretary of state, turned her back on it as a candidate for president.

A failure to enact TPP would represent a significant weakening of the pivot. Kurt M. Campbell, who pushed the policy while he served at Clinton's State Department, called the trade deal the "true sine qua non" — or irreplaceable element — of America's policy in Asia.

Other developments in Asia also raise questions about the success of Obama's pivot. Although Obama had sought to use the policy to reassure Asian leaders that the United States was in

Asia to stay, China appeared to have some success at prying some of America's closest allies from Washington's embrace. In early September 2016, Rodrigo Duterte, the newly elected president of the Philippines, signaled a departure from his nation's long-standing military reliance on the United States, directing his defense secretary to consider buying weapons from China and Russia and announcing that his navy would end joint patrols of the South China Sea with the U.S. Navy. Duterte's shift came despite a ruling by a U.N. arbitration tribunal in The Hague that dismissed China's claims to disputed islands in the South China Sea.

Then there's North Korea, the one country in Asia where Obama did not pivot away from reliance on China. Throughout his two terms, Obama adopted a policy known as "strategic patience" in dealing with the isolated regime, which amounted to hoping that the North would either collapse or be forced into nuclear disarmament by China. Neither occurred. In fact, the pace of North Korean nuclear testing accelerated under the rule of Kim Jong Un.

After North Korea conducted its fifth nuclear test on Sept. 9, Washington and Beijing exchanged accusations over who was to blame for North Korea's growing nuclear arsenal. The reality, though, is that China has been far more committed to the stability of the North Korean regime than to its nuclear containment. Obama's successor will inherit a looming crisis there and one that could very well challenge America's position in Asia.

John Pomfret, a former correspondent for The Washington Post, is the author of the upcoming book "The Beautiful Country and the Middle Kingdom," a history of U.S. relations with China.

President Obama put his frequent-flier miles where his mouth was: Asia

By David Nakamura

President Obama's final foreign trip was a swing through Greece, Germany and Peru just after the 2016 presidential election. It was his 52nd international trip and boosted the number of countries he visited to 58 and the number of days he has spent abroad to 217.

Those numbers are comparable to those of his two most recent predecessors; George W. Bush made 48 trips to 72 countries, and Bill Clinton took 55 trips to 70 countries. But Obama's travel map reveals a noticeable shift in focus, reflecting his stated desire to re-orient more U.S. attention toward Asia.

He put his frequent-flier miles where his mouth was.

Obama made an unprecedented 13 stops in Southeast Asia, a region that the administration believed had been neglected by the United States. At the same time, the president visited fewer countries in Europe and the Middle East than did Bush and Clinton, as he sought to pursue new partnerships and reduce the nation's war footing in Iraq and Afghanistan.

The White House deployed Air Force One strategically to live up to Obama's inaugural address promise in 2009 that under his watch the United States would "extend a hand" to autocratic regimes that were "willing to unclench your fist."

The most notable examples were Burma, also known as Myanmar, and Cuba, where Obama made historic visits to end decades of diplomatic isolation.

Obama also was the first sitting U.S. president to visit Laos and Cambodia in Southeast Asia, as well as Kenya, his father's homeland, and Ethiopia. And he was the first to stop in Malaysia since Lyndon B. Johnson.

Republicans and activist groups criticized the administration for moving too quickly and minimizing human rights abuses, but White House aides defended the approach.

"We have tried to use presidential travel to advance this uniquely Obama effort to address history and hopefully move beyond it," said Ben Rhodes, a White House deputy national security adviser. "Some call it an apology tour, but we call it an effort to open up more space for better relations with different countries. Those are among our most effective trips. People tend to be enormously gratified and surprised that the president of the United States comes to these places."

Presidential travel alone is not enough to reprogram the levers of the federal government's massive national security apparatus. But the Obama White House believed that the president's foreign itinerary would help prod the bureaucracy to shift away from its traditional emphasis on Europe and the Middle East. It wasn't just Obama who traveled more frequently to Asia, but also State Department and Pentagon officials.

For years, U.S. presidents had attended annual trans-Atlantic security and economic summits in Europe. Not long after taking office, the Obama White House proposed something radical: to elevate Southeast Asia to a similar level of importance in the Pacific.

Devoting more of the president's time to that region was not an obvious proposition. The great distances involved required a larger time commitment, and the collection of diverse nations — which featured relatively small economies and divergent political systems — offered no obvious strategic imperative.

But Obama and his aides believed the populous and fast-growing region was increasingly falling under the sway of a rising China.

"There was a conversation among Asian countries that we were not a part of," Rhodes said. "The price of admission was saying the president of the United States would come."

In 2011, after intensive debate inside the White House, Obama announced plans to attend the Association of Southeast Asian Nations (ASEAN) summit and the East Asia Summit each year.

"The downside was: Can we justify committing the president's time to this?" Rhodes said. "And also other regions could object."

Despite competing pressures, the president lived up to his commitment.

Of the 10 countries in ASEAN, Obama visited all but Brunei. All told, he made 13 stops in those nine countries, compared to eight stops in five nations for Bush and five stops in four nations for Clinton.

"When historians look at the 'pivot,' Obama will get the most credit for reengaging Southeast Asia, which has had episodic American attention since the Vietnam War," said Michael Green, who served as senior Asia director at the National Security Council under Bush.

Foreign affairs analysts cautioned that the White House's Asia strategy remains a work in progress, and recent anti-U.S. rhetoric from President Rodrigo Duterte of the Philippines reflects the limits of Obama's personal outreach. Obama visited the Philippines twice — before Duterte was elected — to announce deeper U.S. military and economic partnerships, which Duterte is threatening to reverse.

Still, analysts said the president's visits to countries not accustomed to such attention were generally well received.

"Obama's willingness to go beyond the usual suspects . . . sends a different message to the world of a more open United States that is not locked into old patterns," said Rosa Brooks, a former Pentagon official and contributing editor to Foreign Policy magazine.

Obama did not ignore the major U.S. allies and neighbors. He made 33 stops in seven key countries — France, Germany, the United Kingdom, Canada, Mexico, Japan and South Korea — compared to Bush's 31.

In other cases, however, the White House was willing to curtail Obama's travel to send a different message.

Obama canceled a summit with Russian President Vladimir Putin in Moscow in August 2013 over a series of disputes, including Russia's harboring of former National Security Agency contractor Edward Snowden.

In all, Obama made just two trips to Russia and visited Moscow just once — when Dmitry Medvedev was president in 2009. By comparison, Bush made seven trips to Russia, the most of any country of his presidency, and Clinton made five.

As Obama's tenure winds down, Russia has reemerged as a major geopolitical headache in Ukraine and Syria and on cybersecurity matters. Obama and Putin have met only informally, on the sidelines of global summits.

Obama and Bush have a "different approach to diplomacy," said Thomas Graham, who served as senior Russia director on the National Security Council from 2004 to 2007. Obama "tends to go looking for results. Bush was more about managing the relationship and showing up. This president hasn't had that type of personal relationship with foreign leaders."

Graham said he thinks Obama erred in canceling the summit. But Bush also ultimately failed in his courtship of Putin, and their relationship had deteriorated by the time Bush left office.

Rhodes said that if Medvedev had remained in charge, Obama probably would have made two more trips to Moscow.

"We did not have a real, affirmative agenda to drive with them," he said. "It was symptomatic of a shift under Putin."

Fiona Hill, a Europe expert at the Brookings Institution, said that Obama delegated some diplomatic duties to Vice President Biden in Ukraine and Secretary of State John F. Kerry in Russia. Kerry visited Moscow four times between May 2015 and July 2016.

Aside from Russia, Bush visited 13 other Eastern European nations, including many in the Balkans, where his administration had set up CIA "black site" prisons to house terrorist suspects. Obama has visited just three other countries in that region.

At a recent security conference in Germany, Hill said, European allies made "so much noise about missing President Bush. They missed the backrub: 'Where is the U.S. when you want them?'"

In the Middle East, where his tenure was largely defined by the U.S. invasion of Iraq, Bush visited nine countries and stopped in Iraq four times.

Obama, who opposed the Iraq War and has pulled most U.S. troops out of that nation, has visited five countries in the Middle East, including Iraq only once. (However, Obama made four visits to another war zone — Afghanistan in Central Asia — compared to Bush's two.)

Rhodes said the White House aimed to make up for fewer stops in the Middle East by organizing U.S.-led regional summits that brought Obama together with Persian Gulf leaders in Saudi Arabia and at Camp David.

The administration employed a similar group strategy in Africa, where Obama, the first African American president, visited seven countries to Bush's 11 and Clinton's 10. In August 2014, Obama welcomed more than 50 heads of state to a first-of-its-kind Africa Leaders Summit at the White House.

Asked about the biggest holes on Obama's travel résumé, Rhodes pointed to Nigeria, the richest African nation, and to Sri Lanka, which has made recent democratic reforms.

Foreign policy experts said the next president likely will feel compelled to spend more personal attention on Europe, given Britain's exit from the European Union and Russia's aggression.

But White House aides said they hoped Obama's successor will find a way to maintain his commitment to overlooked parts of the globe.

"Presidential travel sends a huge message," Rhodes said. "A trip can be somewhat transformative."

Obama's presidency brought a dramatic upward shift in America's reputation around the world

By William Wan and Scott Clement

President Obama spent much of his last year in office rejecting a dystopian view of America painted by Republicans. Embedded in Donald Trump's promise to make America great again was a dark portrayal of how the rest of the world now sees the United States: vulnerable, weak and disrespected.

But surveys of global opinion show no major fall-off in perceptions of American power over the past seven years. Indeed, the data points to a dramatic upward shift in America's reputation during the Obama years.

It's hard now to remember just how much antagonism the United States faced across the globe in 2008: People in other countries blamed America for the Iraq war, which undermined support for the war on terrorism. They focused on prisoner treatment at the Abu Ghraib prison in Iraq and talked about America's negative impact on their own countries.

In the final year of George W. Bush's presidency, his abysmal approval ratings at home were matched by the opinions of those abroad.

As a candidate, Obama's promise was to change all that. Almost eight years on, global opinion surveys suggest that, to some degree, he has.

A CHANGE IN OPINION

When the Pew Research Center conducted surveys across 30 countries during Bush's final two years in office, an average of less than 3 in 10 people expressed confidence in Bush. Months later, during Obama's first year in office, more than 6 in 10 expressed such confidence.

That initial surge of approval has barely dipped in the years since — with an average of 61 percent rating Obama positively during the last two years of his presidency in the same countries polled by Pew toward the end of Bush's term. But Obama's popularity and shifts in rhetoric and policy appear to have pulled up global opinion of the United States as a whole.

In 2015 and 2016, an average 60 percent of people throughout the world surveyed by Pew had a favorable opinion of the United States, compared with 49 percent in Bush's final two years in office.

The change in opinion has been sharpest in Western Europe. And Germany in particular shows how dramatic that shift has been.

From 2000 to 2008, the share of Germans who viewed the United States favorably fell by more than half, from 78 to 31 percent. Roughly 7 in 10 Germans wanted the United States to remove troops from Iraq in 2007, and in Bush's final year only 14 percent said they had confidence in his leadership.

Asked to describe this period, Germany's current ambassador to the United States, Peter Wittig, was tactful. "There are many positive things people in Germany associate with Americans," he said. "But in the era of W. Bush, it was mostly, how can I say, overshadowed by the Iraq war."

In the lead-up to the war, hundreds of thousands took to the streets to protest in Berlin and other cities.

"Blood for Oil," screamed the cover of Germany's influential Der Spiegel magazine.

Twice, lawyers filed suits in German courts, trying to prosecute then-Defense Secretary Donald H. Rumsfeld on war crimes.

Even the new American embassy opening in Berlin in 2008

became an opportunity for anti-American bashing, with one German paper calling the upper floors of the embassy the "wellness and waterboarding Area."

Opinions plummeted in other Western countries. In Britain, favorable ratings of the United States fell from 83 to 53 percent from 2000 to 2008. Similar drops were seen in Spain, France, Poland, Turkey, Japan, Indonesia, Mexico and Argentina. By the end of Bush's presidency, the only places left where a majority said they had confidence in how U.S. leaders handled global affairs were Israel and seven countries in sub-Saharan Africa.

It was against that backdrop that Obama arrived in Berlin in 2008, in the middle of the presidential campaign; he was a rock star.

An estimated 200,000 people packed into the Tiergarten park in July 2008 for his speech near the base of Berlin's iconic Victory Column. He promised that if elected president he would put an end to the American unilateralism and cowboy diplomacy that had so incensed Europe. "In Europe, the view that America is part of what has gone wrong in our world ... has become all too common," Obama said. "No one nation, no matter how large or powerful, can defeat such challenges alone."

Trying to explain the emotional reaction of his countrymen back then, Wittig said Obama tapped into something deep in the German psyche.

"You might call it naïve or idealistic," he said. "But it appealed to their hidden love of America ... the idea that America could be a force for good."

"The fact that America could elect an Afro-American. It made America seem avant-garde again. It showed the tremendous strength Americans have," he said.

In Obama's first year, Pew found 93 percent of Germans saying they had confidence in his leadership, according to Pew, a number that has slipped slightly, to 86 percent this year.

VIEWS IN THE MUSLIM WORLD

That success has not been universal.

Obama has barely made a dent, for example, in how the Muslim world views the United States, and opinions in some of those countries have even worsened.

In Pakistan, for example, 62 percent held an unfavorable view of the United States last year, almost identical to the 63 percent in 2008. And 56 percent said they have little or no confidence in Obama's leadership in world affairs, slightly below how they rated Bush in his final year. Obama's use of drone strikes as an anti-terrorism weapon has been widely unpopular.

The last Pew poll available from Egypt in 2014 showed the United States had become even more despised there than during the Bush years. Only 10 percent had a favorable view of the United States in 2013, lower than the 27 percent in 2009 right after Obama took office, and lower than the 22 percent in 2008, Bush's final year.

Much of the debate in the 2016 presidential campaign focused on America's standing in the world, with some candidates and voters expressing worry that the nation's global power had declined. Most of the rest of the world perceived no such fall-off.

When a 2016 Pew survey of 15 countries asked whether America's importance and power has changed in the past decade, a median 41 percent said the United States is similarly powerful as before, while 33 percent said it is less powerful and 20 percent saw it as more powerful.

When it comes to China, global opinion reflects China's rising influence. A median of 43 percent said the United States is still now the world's leading economic power, while 35 percent said China is. With the United States economy's gradual recovery and China's growth rates slowing, the percentage naming the United States as the world's top economy has risen.

CHAPTER 6

THE FIRST FAMILY

'The Obamas came from a place we all came from'

By Wil Haygood

Families can be mysterious, intense and, more often than not, indecipherable to the outside world. Most families seem to endure similar gyrations and upheavals. There are moments of failure and success. There is admirable endurance. To study any individual family is to crisscross tricky terrain, and to invite an endless and almost timeless inquiry.

As Barack, Michelle, Sasha and Malia Obama — the first family, along with grandma Marian Robinson — depart the White House, it is worth looking back at their visage. What did it mean to have a black family, for eight years, astride the political and cultural colossus of American society? How much did the "African" in "African American" resonate?

There perhaps is no other family unit in America that has been analyzed, poked and studied as much as the black family. Its habits, customs, rituals and odyssey have been tabulated, collated and stored for generations. The hyper-curiosity is rooted in slavery and the gouging, sweeping damage it wreaked upon a race of people.

After Emancipation, chroniclers with notebooks traveled far and wide to interview former slaves. They also began showing up after Reconstruction, that halcyon period after the Civil War when blacks were given access to the ballot box and saw the election of black politicians.

In 1936, under the aegis of President Franklin D. Roosevelt's New Deal program, a group of unemployed writers from the Federal

President-elect Barack Obama and his family celebrate his election at Chicago's Grant Park in 2008. (Nikki Kahn/The Washington Post)

Writers Project set out to interview former slaves. For two years, roaming mostly around the southern states, the writers collected more than 2,000 first-person narratives of those who had been held in bondage. The writers would often find themselves emotionally spent after the encounters. Conservative politicians railed against the program, eventually dooming it. But the narratives, now housed at the Library of Congress, endure as testament to what befell black families inside the borders of their own country.

Literature and cinema have also weighed in on the complexities of black family life. On college campuses today, the oral histories from the 1960s — when so much thundering above ground took place — remain quite popular.

The black family has always been fascinating and ripe for study.

But what of a black family that seemingly comes out of nowhere and glides into the White House, against all odds, to preside over a nation? Black families used to have to fight to get a seat at the Woolworth's lunch counter.

Then come Barack and Michelle Obama, president and first lady. What would the presence of this particular family mean to the nation? Given the history of America, what tropes and stereotypes might they upend about the black family?

"The images of this family have been so fortifying for African Americans," says Emily Bernard, a University of Vermont professor and co-author of "Michelle Obama: The First Lady in Photographs." "We've been battling misrepresentation since our arrival into this country: the jezebels, the buffoon. We've been battling all that on a cultural front." She goes on: "In 1951, W.E.B. Du Bois said we need to see positive images of ourselves, and to make a visual narrative for white America to demonstrate our integrity."

Bernard believes the Obamas, as a black family, have accomplished something notable in the annals of White House living.

"You can't fake how much joy they take in each other as a family," she says. "Malia and Sasha have the burden to represent the race. And they're exceptional and normal at the same time. The family is not scandalous. Those girls are delightfully ordinary."

Like many, Bernard has been growing wistful about the Obama family departing the White House. "My grandmother said no way a black man could be president. She couldn't see the potential," Bernard recalls. "It's truly amazing. A lot of people sacrificed so I could teach at the University of Vermont. For us with brown skin, we are descendants from that generation. The Obamas came from a place we all came from."

Bernard has also noted the cultural flourishes the Obamas have brought to the White House, leaving her feeling that they did not forget their roots. "President Obama has maintained a soulfulness I don't think we've seen in a modern presidency," she says.

IN THE PUBLIC EYE

The America that bothered to notice got its first sustained visual glimpse of the black family — sitting together, in calm repose — by looking upon daguerreotypes published after the Civil War. They were photos of reunited black families, brought together before the camera lens to celebrate life and freedom in the era of Jubilee.

President Obama after taking the oath of office in the Blue Room of the White House on Jan. 20, 2013. Daughters Malia and Sasha and U.S. Supreme Court Chief Justice John Roberts were also present. (Pool photo by Doug Mills/Getty Images)

President Obama and the first lady kiss at Verizon Center during a Team USA exhibition game against Brazil in July 2012. (Toni L. Sandys/The Washington Post)

President Obama crosses the Edmund Pettus Bridge with some prominent figures to mark the 50th anniversary of the "Bloody Sunday" march in Selma, Ala. (Jacquelyn Martin/Associated Press)

The figures in the photos couldn't help but look exhausted in their often ill-fitting clothes.

In the looming years, the struggle remained monumental. Segregation sat the black family on the wrong side of the railroad tracks, from community to community, for decades. Black newspapers, battling to stay alive, often bent their focus toward black dysfunction. Crime sold plenty of copies of the Chicago Defender, the Baltimore Afro-American, the New York Amsterdam News. The black family, beyond its own black-oriented publications — which rarely wound up in white households — seemed almost other-worldly.

It can seem daunting to set the Obama family outside the White House, to envision them being compared to mortals.

"I think the narrative of the Obama family may be," says Gerald Early, a professor at Washington University in St. Louis and director of its Center for Humanities, "that some people will look at them and say, 'They're the exception. They're not the typical black family.' The response to that by many black people will be, 'Here is the black family to aspire to. Here is a black father contributing to his loving family.' And still other blacks will say, 'We know a lot of other black families like the Obamas. It's just that people haven't noticed them because they've been focusing on the dysfunctional part of black family life.'"

That has been an issue for many decades — and one that black artists have worked to address. One of the more memorable looks at black family life in modern times took place on a Broadway stage in 1959. The play was "A Raisin in the Sun," written by Lorraine Hansberry. Hansberry was born in Chicago, where Michelle Obama was born and where Barack Obama began his political career.

The Hansberry drama was about a poor black Chicago family and how a $10,000 life insurance check would test the moral courage and steadfastness of various family members. Just before the play opened on Broadway in the spring of 1959, Hansberry wrote a letter to her mother. "Mama, it is a play that tells the truth about people, Negroes and life and I think it will help a lot of people to understand how we are just as complicated as they are — and just as mixed up — but above all, that we have among our miserable and downtrodden ranks — people who are the very essence of human dignity."

The president and first lady had a much-publicized "date night" in 2014, when they ventured to Broadway to see the revival of "A Raisin in the Sun," which starred, among others, Denzel Washington, Sophie Okonedo and Anika Noni Rose.

America is still struggling to embrace the "human dignity" of African Americans reflected in Hansberry's play. Early says he believes that as the years roll forward, President Obama will be central to that. He believes Obama will assume the mantle — whether he wishes it for himself or not — of the premiere black father figure, replacing the scandal-tarred, fictional father played by Bill Cosby on his long-running TV show. "Obama will have that role even more now," he says.

President Obama's post-presidency plans are bountiful. A gifted writer, he will turn attention to his memoirs. There is the presidential library to attend to. But his prayed-for attention to black America will be robust, and a plea he is apt to answer quickly. His unprecedented 2015 visit to a federal penitentiary in Oklahoma struck a chord among black families, all too many of whom have been touched, in some way, by the criminal justice system.

Obama's effort to explain to white America the heartbreak of black families when Trayvon Martin, black and unarmed, was shot and killed in Florida by a neighborhood watch volunteer who was acquitted of all charges was palpable and searing. In a nation that has never had a candid conversation about race — unlike South Africa after apartheid, with its Truth and Reconciliation Commission — he will find himself expected to play the role of shaman, poet, conciliator and statesman.

Many expect Michelle Obama to also play an active role in the discourse that relates to the nation's well-being. She has been an advocate for women's rights, healthy eating and civility.

'POSITIVE REVERBERATIONS'

In 2006, then-Sen. Barack Obama rolled into Columbus, Ohio, to gauge his presidential prospects. He met Donna James, a business executive, and her husband, Larry James, a partner at a law firm that bears his name. They hosted a gathering for Obama. "He was just a normal, thoughtful human being," recalls Donna James, whom Obama would later appoint chairman of the National Women's Business Council. James watched Obama and his family lay their impress upon the White House. She says she was struck by the couple's decision to bring Marian Robinson, Michelle's mother, to the White House with them.

"It was out of this sense of family," James says. "It's out of black culture. Latino people do the same thing. It was a loving family thing to do, and also very smart."

There is little doubt that the Obamas represented a boon to the spread of blackness out into mainstream American society. Some wonder whether this hid a sea of white resentment, giving way to the racially charged campaign and election of Donald Trump.

Hollywood has not been known as an inclusive laboratory for black-oriented films. But with the Obamas in the White House, there was a noticeable uptick in cinematic diversity. Films such as "The Butler," "Fruitvale Station," "Selma" and, most recently, "Southside With You," about Barack Obama's courtship of Michelle Robinson, all elicited a conversational line pointing back to the White House and its occupants.

"One level of the positive reverberations and interest in black history is because of Michelle and her kids," says Peniel Joseph, a historian and professor of public affairs at the University of Texas at Austin. "For elites — artists — Obama was the best thing that ever happened. You found a lot more people interested in black life."

Joseph says the complexity of President Obama's family background — white American mother, black Kenyan father — was something that was easily digestible to many blacks. "Blacks know people with Africans in their family," he offers. "And black folks just loved the way Michelle looked. In their mind, someone like Obama [a Harvard Law School grad] often married white women."

Obama not only married a black woman, but married one proud of her black heritage; Joseph feels that invigorated discussions about black family life. Although the Obamas hosted a variety of musical events at the White House — country, blues, rock — it did not go unnoticed by blacks that the pride seemed to swell with a kind of warm cultural magic when the likes of Al Green, Smokey Robinson and Esperanza Spalding were in the White House. After all, there was a time when black minstrel acts were the only black entertainment seen inside the White House.

"Because of Michelle's family," adds Joseph, "you see how family structure is quintessential to understanding the black family: There is slavery, freedom, the Great Migration, and out of all that, you somehow carve a space in America to have kids and are able to make a way for those kids to make it to Princeton."

Michelle Obama is a Princeton graduate.

Joseph also says the mere presence of the Obama family on the national stage keeps manifesting itself in a nation's dialogue. "Bill O'Reilly said that slaves were well fed, as if he had dined out with slaves," says Joseph, referring to the TV commentator. Joseph feels such raw commentary — seen as offensive to many across the racial landscape — was loosed because of the presence of Obama. "Many people made a secret covenant that with Obama elected, institutional racism was over. Instead, by electing the first black president, we all got deeper into the narrative of racism and slavery. In a lot of ways, certain white people feel betrayed by Obama because they felt once he was elected, Obama wouldn't have to talk about race. But we're seeing more examples of late, like Georgetown University coming to grips with slavery."

The university recently announced it would find ways to aid the descendants of the 272 slaves it once sold to keep the school afloat. The school also announced other measures, such as a slavery exhibit and a memorial to those slaves linked to the school.

If, at times, the everyday presence of a black American family in the nation's mind-set has seemed to unleash forces both good and not so good, there are some things that will resonate and be spoken of for generations to come: A black father as president walked his girls hand-in-hand across the lawn of the most powerful address in the world. A black mother gazed at that tableau and took herself back to the stories of beaten-down slaves who once tilled the White House lawns where her husband and daughters loped — and she then became fearless in letting the world know the gritty dream-like magic of such a scene. And a black grandmother — Lorraine Hansberry's "Mama" all through these eight long history- defying years — looked out from her own White House window upon it all. A woman who stayed silent to the world, her presence an echo back over the years of America and the black family.

Haygood is a journalist, professor and author known for his 2008 Washington Post article "A Butler Well Served by This Election," about Eugene Allen. The movie "The Butler" was based on his story.

How Michelle Obama became
a singular American voice

By Peter Slevin

Three weeks after Inauguration Day in 2009 and still a long way from crafting an agenda, Michelle Obama climbed into her motorcade and paid a visit to Mary's Center, a Latino community services agency a few miles north of the White House. She read "Brown Bear, Brown Bear, What Do You See?" to the young children and met with teenagers who asked why she had come.

The first reason, she said, was that Washington was now the Obamas' home and they had always been taught to listen and not just pass on by. The second reason identified the audience and framed the approach that would define this most uncommon first lady's agenda for the next eight years.

"I think it's real important for young kids, particularly kids who come from communities without resources, to see me, not the first lady," she said. "To see that there is no magic to me sitting here. There are no miracles that happen. There is no magic dust."

With the 13 teenagers seated in a semicircle, Obama shared the setbacks and self-doubt she faced as the daughter of black working-class parents in Chicago. When people told her she couldn't achieve something, she set out to prove them wrong. One step at a time, she climbed, and now she felt an obligation to share.

"When you get, you give back," she said.

Obama would give much bigger speeches on much bigger stages as she became one of the most famous people in the world. For many Democrats, she was the moral voice of the 2016 presidential campaign, calling out Republican Donald Trump for trafficking in "prejudice, fears and lies." For other fans, she was simply the first lady who went viral, making them smile with her eclectic fashion choices and her energetic, sometimes goofy pitches for healthier eating.

The heart of Obama's efforts, however, was a message about the persistent inequities of race, class and gender in America. In scores of speeches and projects, she turned again and again to the stacked deck. These were the themes and conundrums that animated her work before she reached the White House and now seem certain to shape her choices after she departs.

For all the grief she took from critics who conjured radicalism, grievance or, bizarrely, racism from her finely tuned remarks, Obama's antidotes were fundamentally timeless and conservative. More than anything, she used the strength of her own Chicago-to-Princeton-to-the-White-House narrative to urge kids to believe in themselves and never quit. She mastered the levers of popular culture and harnessed the convening power of her office and her carefully curated brand to establish partnerships with the private sector.

Obama addressed obesity, which disproportionately affects low-income families and children of color. She worked to increase arts education in poorly performing schools and ease the path for aspiring first-generation college students. She dispensed hugs to thousands of children, saying in a simple embrace that she believed in them. At a BET special, she called out, "Black girls rock!"

A straight-talker by temperament, she modulated her tone in deference to the role. Eternally disciplined and pragmatic, she never swung for the fences. Critics on the left chided her for not being bold enough, as she acknowledged last year. Her answer: "These were my choices, my issues, and I decided to tackle them in the way that felt most authentic to me — in a way that was both substantive and strategic, but also fun and, hopefully, inspiring."

When Obama took up her unpaid job three days after her 45th birthday, she faced vast and conflicting expectations. She was

First lady Michelle Obama addresses the Democratic National Convention in Philadelphia on July 25, 2016. (Jabin Botsford/The Washington Post)

Children hug Michelle Obama as she visits Mary's Center, a D.C. non-profit organization that helps people with limited access to health services, in 2009. (Nicholas Kamm/Agence France-Presse via Getty Images)

Michelle Obama exercises with children from Orr Elementary School in Washington, D.C., on Sept. 6, 2013. (Marvin Joseph/The Washington Post)

the first African American first lady in a country that was anything but post-racial. She was the magnetic campaigner who told audiences that power concedes nothing without a struggle. She was the highly educated, professionally accomplished mother of two young daughters who smilingly adopted the moniker of "mom in chief."

"From the moment we walked in the door, people have wanted to get inside her head and figure her out. 'Is she in this box or that box? Why isn't she doing this or doing that?'" said Jocelyn Frye, a Harvard Law School friend who became Obama's first policy adviser. "She's not a person who lives in boxes. It's just not that simple."

HER ROAD TO THE WHITE HOUSE

The personal story that Obama carried into the White House in January 2009 was enough to etch her name in the history books even if she did not accomplish anything more. She called herself "the little black girl from the South Side of Chicago." As she would say later, her ancestors had arrived in the United States in chains and now she and Barack Obama were living in a home that slaves helped build.

But in other ways, too, Obama brought a set of experiences markedly different from her modern-day predecessors. Of the previous eight presidents, four had been governors, four had been vice presidents. Their wives had lived in the public eye. Obama was a young Chicago professional, a working mother in a big city who spoke openly about juggling jobs, chores and child-rearing with her increasingly famous and preoccupied husband.

By upbringing, she was urban and attuned to issues of prejudice, hardship and inequality. She adored her father, Fraser C. Robinson III, a gregarious aspiring artist who spent his working life as a shift worker in the city water plant. A swimmer, boxer and soldier as a young man, he was diagnosed with multiple sclerosis in his 30s. His health deteriorated, and he went from one crutch to two to a motorized cart. He died in 1991 at age 55, still working at the plant.

Both of Obama's grandfathers had come north in the Great Migration, and many members of the Robinson and Shields families lived nearby. Purnell Shields, a talented carpenter and Obama's maternal grandfather, was barred as an African American from the labor unions that claimed the highest-paying jobs. Fraser C. Robinson Jr. spent much of his career as a postal worker. If he had been born white, Obama once said, he would have been a banker.

Obama spent time with this extended family. She knew them all, from those who were prospering to those who were ailing or just getting by. She also knew countless schoolmates who seemed hardly different from her, yet had fallen short of their ambitions. When Barack Obama met her in 1989, he detected a sense of vulnerability that he traced to Michelle's sense that life was "terrifyingly random." She called herself "a statistical anomaly."

After ditching the prosperous law firm, where she found the work soulless and many colleagues narrow, she spent two years doing economic development work at City Hall with future White House adviser Valerie Jarrett. Next, in what she described as the happiest phase of her working life, she built the Chicago office of Public Allies, a nonprofit leadership training program with roots in community organizing.

Next, she spent a dozen years as an administrator at the University of Chicago, where she elevated the interests of neighboring African American communities. Much as she would in the White House, she searched for ways to connect a powerful and often remote institution with communities where it could do some good. Comfortable and connected in both worlds, she saw herself as a bridge.

In 2001, protesters seeking more construction jobs for African Americans at the university medical center said she should be fired. One said Obama and her colleagues were looking out for themselves and did "not have the best interests of blacks at heart." Obama persisted. In the next seven years, 42.9 percent of the hospital's spending on new construction, or $48.8 million, went to firms run by minorities or women, according to university figures.

The focus was not new. At Harvard Law School, where the tenured faculty was 96 percent white and 92 percent male, Obama spoke up for greater diversity. Charles Ogletree, a mentor and professor, pinpointed her passions early.

"Everything she wrote, the things that she was involved in, the things that she thought about," he recalled of her law school years in the mid-1980s, "were in effect reflections on race and gender. And how she had to keep the doors open for women and men going forward."

A PORTFOLIO OF PASSIONS

One of Obama's signatures was the push for a seat at the table — or in "the room where it happens," to borrow from "Hamilton," the Broadway musical the Obamas admire. A few years ago, she told a gathering of White House interns that if they were not prepared to risk their power when they claimed that seat, they needed to make room for someone who would.

In reaching the most rarefied of tables, she figured she had four years, maybe eight, to make something happen, to "move the needle," as she put it. As the media made a fuss over a new hairstyle, she once explained how she saw the role of first lady: "We take our bangs and we stand in front of important things that the world needs to see. And, eventually, people stop looking at the bangs and they start looking at what we're standing in front of."

Obama saw early that she could connect with disadvantaged young people by describing her South Side upbringing and the choices she made in her life. Even as the Obamas set out unambiguously to be the president and first lady for the entire country, they were determined "to look out for people who historically have not had people looking out for them," Valerie Jarrett said in an interview. "Certainly, African American women and girls see themselves in her in a unique way."

The White House portfolio included Let's Move, her childhood obesity project, and efforts to open the White House and its grounds to kids who barely knew where it was and never imagined stepping inside. She established Joining Forces to help the military and their families with jobs and workplace issues and started a small mentoring program that became a personal cause.

She worked on homelessness among veterans and pushed Reach Higher, seeking to increase post-secondary education for low-income adolescents. Finally, she launched Let Girls Learn, an international initiative designed to improve access to secondary school for millions of girls around the world who found themselves on the outside looking in.

Throughout, Obama made clear to her staff that she favored coherent projects backed by creative but realistic thinking. She sought buy-in from federal agencies, state governments and private partners, and she wanted to make use of every opportunity. She told her aides, "Don't just put me on a plane, send me someplace and have me smile."

"She never looked at things esoterically or theoretically. It was practical and real," said Democratic strategist Stephanie Cutter, who advised her at key moments. "Her focus was never 'How do I move Washington?' It was much bigger than that. It was 'How do you mobilize a country? How are real people outside of Washington going to see things?'"

At the White House, she staged arts events, from dance, music and spoken word to food and design workshops. She made sure that artists who were performing for well-heeled East Room audiences at night were teaching children at the White House or local schools during the day. Her tastes tilted to designers, artists, playwrights and directors of color, choices that alerted millions of Obama-watchers to work they might not have seen or heard.

In 2011, she helped launch Turnaround Arts, a program designed to deliver arts teaching, inspiration and supplies to some of the worst-performing schools in the country — often in places where arts programming was a budget casualty. From eight pilot programs in 2011, the project now reaches 68 schools, with 20 to be added in 2017.

"She knows the power of the arts. It's visceral and it's who she is," said Megan Beyer, executive director of the President's Committee on the Arts and Humanities. "Every time we do an event, she'll look at the audience and she'll say, 'This is not a fluke. This is what happens when you invest in these kids.'"

To critics on the right, including former Alaska governor Sarah Palin, who mocked or denounced new science-based standards for school lunches as overly intrusive, Obama urged them to look more closely. She pointed to the millions of low-income children who depend on those meals and the federal government's help in paying for them.

"We simply can't afford to say, 'Oh, well, it's too hard, so let's not do it,'" Obama said in 2014. When lobbyists persuaded Congress to count one-eighth of a cup of tomato paste in pizza sauce as the equivalent of a half-cup of vegetables, she wrote dismissively in the New York Times, "You don't have to be a nutritionist to know that this doesn't make much sense."

PRESERVING NORMALCY

Inside the East Wing, Obama commanded intense loyalty from her staff and set her own agenda, down to the number of public days on her schedule — two at first, while Malia and Sasha were getting settled, and later three. She stayed closer to home than Laura Bush and Hillary Clinton, who each traveled abroad more than twice as much, and put limits on her campaign trips, especially when not campaigning for her husband.

She tightly controlled her message. In eight years, she never gave a news conference, although she held a select few roundtables with reporters. She rarely granted interviews to the beat reporters who knew her work the best. More often, and more strategically, she granted face time to grateful personalities and comedians, along with media outlets carefully chosen for the audiences they reached.

President Obama and the first lady, along with their guests, wear 3-D glasses at a Super Bowl party at the White House in 2009. (Pete Souza/The White House)

The first family prepares to board Air Force One on Aug. 21, 2016, after their vacation on Martha's Vineyard, in Massachusetts. (Steven Senne/Associated Press)

Michelle Obama blows kisses to graduates after delivering the commencement address for Bowie State University, a historically black university, in Maryland in May 2013. (Chip Somodevilla/Getty Images)

Aides and friends were barely more accessible. When reporters called, former chief of staff Jackie Norris once said, Obama expected her friends to "check in and have conversations and make sure that it's good for her." Mostly, the friends did.

Since the beginning of the first presidential campaign nearly 10 years ago, Obama has credited her girlfriends with keeping her grounded amid the maelstrom. "When you're isolated, that's when you need your girls. They can keep you together when no one else can," said Angela Kennedy, a D.C. public defender and former Princeton roommate who sees Obama regularly. "She's smart. She recognized that."

Not trailed by the presidential press pool, Obama escaped to the gym, restaurants, theaters and her friends' houses, as well as the occasional trip to the presidential retreat at Camp David. It helped to have her mother, Marian Robinson, now 79, living on the third floor of the White House. "I can always go up to her room and cry, complain, argue," Obama said. "And she just says, go on down there and do what you're supposed to do."

Obama spoke often of what it meant to have normal family dinners and activities with Malia and Sasha, talking about the girls' doings and keeping things light. She has always been able "to stay above the fray," said Frye, her Harvard friend, in part by "meeting with real people and talking about real-world problems. At the end of the day, she has kept her head."

Obama's ascendance — as mother, mentor, leader and critic — carries many meanings in American culture, particularly as an African American woman, said Nell Irvin Painter, an emeritus professor of American history at Princeton.

"Her power is a symbolic power," Painter said, noting the way Obama "has conducted herself as first lady. She has grace, there is no question, but I would add elegance. It's a kind of assurance that is also something new for a black woman in public life. She is the symbol of what an American can be. Michelle Obama has presented a universal American identity."

A VOICE ON RACE AND RACISM

On May 9, 2015, Obama took the stage at Tuskegee University in Alabama and delivered the most thorough and personal speech about race and racism of her tenure. As a speechmaker, said author Garry Wills, who won a Pulitzer Prize for his study of Lincoln's Gettysburg Address, "I don't know that she has any competitors in women's history." She wowed millions of fans with keynote addresses at three successive Democratic National Conventions, but she also had a serious body of work that received less attention in mainstream circles.

Many times before her Tuskegee appearance, she had spoken about the country's history of violence and discrimination against African Americans. She did it in Orangeburg, S.C., in 2007 to woo black support for her husband's candidacy. She did it in Nashville during the 2012 reelection campaign, and in Topeka, Kan., in 2014 to mark the 60th anniversary of *Brown v. Board of Education*. And she did it at other historically black universities, including Bowie State, Jackson State and North Carolina A&T.

Together, the talks reflected a lifetime of thinking about the shifting landscape of racism, the advances and the setbacks. At Tuskegee, she spoke of slights and hurdles while suggesting strategies — tested by her own experience, as always — to block out the noise and navigate a path forward.

"Here's the thing: The road ahead is not going to be easy," she told the graduates in an address that tracked the history of the Tuskegee Airmen, a storied black flying squadron in World War II. "It never is, especially for folks like you and me. Because while we've come so far, the truth is that those age-old problems are stubborn and they haven't fully gone away. So there will be times, just like for those Airmen, when you feel like folks look right past you or they see just a fraction of who you are."

"Too many folks feel frustrated and invisible," Obama said. She cited worries about being pulled over "for absolutely no reason," or being overlooked for a job "because of the way your name sounds," or sending children to schools "that may no longer be separate, but are far from equal." Above all, she said, there is the "realization that no matter how far you rise in life, how hard you work to be a good person, a good parent, a good citizen, for some folks, it will never be enough."

The Obamas were not immune, despite their efforts, their achievements, their conduct. For years, Donald Trump sowed doubts about Barack Obama's birth and citizenship, while talk show host Rush Limbaugh told his millions of followers that Michelle suffered from "uppity-ism" and called her "Michelle My Butt." Foes likened her to a character from Planet of the Apes, a Star Wars Wookiee and a gorilla, a racist slur with a particularly long and ugly history. They challenged her patriotism and even questioned her gender.

But no matter how grim the outlook and how significant the structural challenges, Obama said at Tuskegee, despair and anger are "not an excuse to just throw up our hands and give up." Instead, she proposed the measured, practical, traditional responses that had worked for her. Study, organize, band together, be a mentor, help a cousin fill out a financial aid form and "vote, vote, vote."

"You have got everything you need to do this. You've got it in you," she said in her best I-believe-in-you tone. "Most of all, you've got yourselves and all of the heart, grit and smarts that got you to this day."

It was never Obama's style to summon people to the barricades. She drew criticism from some African American intellectuals and activists for perpetuating a bootstraps narrative that said black people must be twice as good to do just as well as whites. Painter recognized the critique but saw Obama's message differently.

"She also says you can figure it out. That's a crucial part," Painter said. "Her commentary to black kids is, 'You can do it. It's not just lecturing and shaking her finger in their faces, but an encouragement. It's pragmatic, but the way she phrases it, it is full of empathy and I think there is still a lack of empathy in the way the United States speaks to black people."

Michelle Obama campaigns with Hillary Clinton in Winston-Salem, N.C., on Oct. 27, 2016. (Melina Mara/The Washington Post)

The response to Obama's remarks provided proof aplenty. Conservative talk show host Laura Ingraham saw "a litany of victimization." Media comment boards filled with talk of a "tirade" and an "America-hater" and an "angry woman who has no appreciation for the many gifts our country has bestowed on her." Someone wrote, "Can she or her husband ever just be Americans? Why do they always have to focus on their skin color? Repulsive."

But also, "Michelle for President!" — something that Obama, whose favorability ratings routinely topped 60 percent, has said will never happen. "No. Nope. Not going to do it," she said earlier this year.

ASSESSING AMERICA

Michelle Obama was dismayed by the rise of Donald Trump. She perceived danger in the candidacy of an unstudied Republican who lied with abandon and routinely mocked and disparaged rivals, critics and entire swathes of the American populace, all the while vowing to wreck much of what the Obama administration spent eight years building.

"This is not normal. This is not politics as usual," Obama declared at an October rally in New Hampshire after a tape surfaced of Trump boasting about grabbing women by the genitals. A growing number of women said they had been accosted. "I know it's a campaign, but this isn't about politics. It's about human decency. It's about right and wrong."

Obama said repeatedly during the campaign that Trump was dangerous, undeserving and lacking "any idea what this job takes." In Philadelphia, she pointedly recalled Trump's leadership of the birther movement, referring to the "hurtful, deceitful questions deliberately designed to undermine" her husband's presidency.

The attacks on Trump were the strongest, sharpest words Obama uttered in public during the White House years. Whatever her anger or dismay, she never said she was surprised, for these were the regressive forces that she had seen in action her entire life.

On a weekday morning, with not many people watching, Obama delivered her take on the political moment. To a rapt church audience — men and women, white and black — she said in a tone more suited to a seminar than a rally, "My fear is that we don't know what truth looks like anymore." She spoke of her hard-won understanding of the world, drawing on her Chicago life, where persistence and good intentions came with no guarantees.

Politicians had become expert at turning doubt into fear, she said, as life got "harder, progressively harder, for regular people."

"We're still a nation that's a little too mean," Obama said. "I wish mean worked, because we're good at it. Our tone is bad and we've grown to believe that, somehow, mean talk is tough talk ... and we reward it. Not just in politics, but we reward it in every sliver of our culture. We look on people who are tough and say, 'That's what we need.'"

Obama spoke those words in South Carolina in January 2008. As Trump makes his way to Washington with his gilded pitchfork, her assessment rings true for more than 62 million Americans who supported him and millions more who didn't care enough to vote. She is leaving the White House with work unfinished and fresh troubles brewing. She was right that day at Mary's Center, in her first weeks on the job, when she offered a verdict that applied as much to the nation as to herself. There are no miracles, no magic dust.

What Obama offered was something else. To audiences great and small, she presented conviction, savvy, a dose of inspiration and a certain faith that the battles were worth waging and the effort would pay off in the end.

Peter Slevin, a former Post national correspondent, is the author of "Michelle Obama: A Life."

How the Obamas leveraged fame
to advance a political agenda

By Krissah Thompson

Will the United States ever again have a president who drops the mic or a first lady who raps about going to college?

Barack and Michelle Obama were arguably more conversant in popular culture than any other couple who has occupied the White House. After eight years, they have become full-fledged celebrities, warmly embraced by America's two arbiters of modern cool: Hollywood and hip-hop.

It has been a two-way street.

The Obamas are lovers of pop culture and have used it to communicate in ways that are rare among political figures.

They show up constantly on television, reference popular music and use artists who produce that music to promote their agenda — all while making it clear they're in on the game.

In the final summer of his administration, President Obama sat on a stool with a deadpan look on his face as he slow-jammed the news with late-night host Jimmy Fallon; it was the president's second time doing the segment.

The first lady hopped in a car with comedian James Corden for his popular "Carpool Karaoke" bit. There she rapped with Missy Elliott to a pop song recorded to support a White House initiative to boost girls' education. Then they both sang Elliott's hit "Get Your Freak On."

For many, the Obamas' middle-aged hipness has been a breath

of fresh air and smart politics. For others, all that exposure was unseemly and tarnished the presidency.

"The president has always had an appeal beyond the political world, even back to the 2008 campaign when he was brushing his shoulders off," said Democratic strategist Jamal Simmons.

"The job description for how to attain the nation's highest public office is similar to the job description for show business," Simmons added. "You've got to hit your marks. You've got to be a good communicator."

Some disagreed. The first time the president slow-jammed the news he was running for reelection, and former Fox News host Gretchen Carlson said that appearing on comedy shows "lowers the status of the office."

Michelle Obama's surprise appearance at the 2013 Academy Awards to present the Best Picture award via satellite also prompted some criticism.

"She's as glamorous as any other star, [and] she is comfortable in that role," Anita McBride, who served as chief of staff to first lady Laura Bush and is now an executive in residence at American University, said at the time. "As far as the optics in the national conversation, you can see where the other half have come down, 'Is this really necessary?'"

PLAYING TO THEIR STRENGTHS

The trendy and often trending Obamas presided over an unprecedented cultural climate change. Social media wasn't a cultural force when they entered the White House. As they prepared to leave, it had become the arena hosting the country's most vigorous conversations, political and otherwise. And urban culture, with its tilt toward black celebrities, dominates the national arts scene.

In many ways, they have been a president and first lady suited for such a cultural moment. Theirs is one of the youngest first families in the nation's history, and the first African American. As such, they were going to be a different kind of first family by default.

Their connection to popular culture has only added another layer to that narrative of difference.

Early on, Obama's political opponents picked up on the risks of his pop-culture cachet. When his wife gave him a fist bump after he secured the Democratic presidential nomination in 2008, it was pounced on by critics; a Fox News host wondered whether it was a "terrorist fist jab." Other Americans, who recognized the fist pound from hip-hop culture, rolled their collective eyes at the negative interpretation.

About that same time, Obama's Republican rival, Sen. John McCain, ran a campaign ad called "Celeb," branding Obama as "the biggest celebrity in the world" and comparing him to Britney Spears and Paris Hilton. The critique lingered: Do you want to talk to famous people, or do you want to solve the problems of a dangerous world?

Obama and his strategists determined the question to be outdated. They thought they could leverage his fame to push their agenda. Just a few months after his inauguration, he made history as the first sitting president to appear on a late-night talk show when he went on "The Tonight Show With Jay Leno" to tout his economic agenda.

"You can't just do the one print interview or the one sit-down television interview or even the one interview that's going to be on the Web," said Jon Lovett, a former Obama speechwriter. "You have to find people where they are, and they are getting their information from a lot of different places, including entertainment.

"We as a culture have decided that we want our political figures to speak to us through not just totally dry and boring" channels, he added. "We want to get a sense of them as people through comedy shows and personal interviews, along with everything else."

Other presidents had appeared on late-night shows and comedy programs while running for office, but most stopped once they were in the Oval Office.

"Sitting presidents didn't do that," said Robert Thompson, the founding director of the Bleier Center for Television and Popular Culture at Syracuse University.

Richard Nixon was helped by his appearance on "Rowan & Martin's Laugh-In" as a candidate. Jack Kennedy went on "Tonight Starring Jack Paar" when he ran for office. Bill Clinton memorably played the sax on Arsenio Hall's show. But other appearances on popular television were few, Thompson said.

Obama kept it going because he and his team thought it played to his strengths, said Stephanie Cutter, who has been a top adviser to both of the Obamas. The late-night appearances "were incredibly effective not just in reaching people, but in communicating that then-Senator Obama was a real person and likable, and that likability and trust went a long way when things got tough, like during the financial crisis," she said.

The president has a dry wit. Michelle Obama is "just funny," said Cutter, who helped create the first lady's Let's Move! program.

"In terms of message delivery, you don't always have to hit people over the head with a stick. It can come through comedy and skits, [but] not every politician or public figure has the skill set to do it."

EXPERIMENTING WITH MEDIA

Michelle Obama's East Wing office became a kind of laboratory for experimenting with new media.

After her 2008 speech at the Democratic National Convention, media requests started pouring in, Cutter said, and the future first lady began to develop a media profile.

She posted childhood photos on Instagram. Her number of followers there surpassed the number following the main White House account. And her staff built partnerships with Internet stars on YouTube and Vine, some of whom visited Washington to make silly videos with the first lady.

"I view myself as being the average woman," Obama told Variety this summer. "While I am first lady, I wasn't first lady my whole life. I'm a product of pop culture. I'm a consumer of pop culture, and I know what resonates with people. I know what they'll get a chuckle out of and what they think is kind of silly. And whenever my team approaches me with ideas and concepts, we're usually like, 'Is this really funny? Are people going to understand it?' "

The president has given his wife credit for taking chances. Before he sat down with Zach Galifianakis on "Between Two Ferns" to make a pitch for young people to sign up for the Affordable Care Act, the first lady had a push-up contest with Ellen DeGeneres to promote fitness.

"Michelle understood this earlier, because she had fewer resources," the president said in the New York Times magazine this year. "You have to leverage different platforms because a fireside chat just gets lost in the noise today. People aren't part of one conversation; they're part of a million. You're drawing on where the culture is to get the message out."

Often, the television hosts and celebrities who helped the Obamas push their policy and political messages received invitations to White House parties that became the talk of the town. DeGeneres attended several, as did Beyoncé, her husband Jay Z and the actor Tom Hanks. At the president's 50th birthday party, which was held at the executive mansion, they danced alongside government officials, including Vice President Biden and then-Treasury Secretary Timothy Geithner.

"I felt like I died and went to black heaven," comedian Chris Rock said of that party. Rock recounted the experience in a stand-up routine: As the party went on, he said, the music got "blacker and blacker." The DJ played Beyoncé's "Crazy in Love," and Malia and Sasha started dancing, he said. "They came from out of nowhere and . . . started doing the Dougie."

Partying with celebs reinforced the Obamas' pop culture cachet, and their manner of communicating with the country changed expectations for how a president and first lady should behave, said Amanda Miller Littlejohn, a public relations and personal branding consultant.

"You saw the White House in the past as being this untouchable, unrelatable institution," Miller Littlejohn said, adding that pop culture and the presidency may now be permanently linked.

The 2016 race for president, too, reflected this. The winner, Donald Trump, was aided by his past as a reality television star. Media critics said his political rise was due, in part, to his ability to dominate the pop-culture conversation.

#ThanksObama.

For the Obamas, looking cool is part of the job

By Robin Givhan

There was something intriguing about Barack and Michelle Obama that went beyond their historic rise to power. It was, in part, their manner of being, their aesthetic and the nonverbal ways in which they communicated — with the public and with each other. Their physical language and style spoke intimately to African Americans, but they also broadly reflected the contemporary culture.

The fist bump: It was not a romantic gesture. It was a gesture of friendship and solidarity. The Obamas were teammates standing eye to eye, in it together. The fist bump came deep into the 2008 presidential campaign, when Obama was closing in on the Democratic nomination. It signaled youthfulness, athleticism and street cool. In the body language of mainstream politics, it was a new idiom for communicating encouragement and satisfaction. But because it wasn't the political cliche — hands joined, arms raised in victory — it attracted attention, speculation and suspicion. Was there more to this gesture than met the eye? Change was afoot. New voices and a different demographic were ascendant.

Embrace: The emotion was palpable but contained. Michelle Obama had her arms stretched around his neck. His eyes were closed and his arms, with their shirtsleeves rolled up, were wrapped tightly around her waist. Barack Obama embraced his wife in a bear hug on stage during a campaign stop in Iowa during his bid for reelection in 2012. He had not seen her in days. He was

Sen. Barack Obama and his wife, Michelle Obama, fist bump during a rally at the Xcel Energy Center in St. Paul, Minn., in June 2008. (Scott Olson/Getty Images)

Barack Obama ✓
@BarackObama

2+ Follow

r more years.

ETS LIKES
287 618,375

President Obama and first lady Michelle Obama embrace during a campaign stop. The tweet, following the 2012 election, was the most shared photo on Twitter for a while. (@BarackObama via Twitter)

President Obama and first lady Michelle Obama take the stage for their first dance at the Neighborhood Ball in 2009 in celebration of his inauguration. (Richard A. Lipski/The Washington Post)

Michelle Obama and daughter Malia walk off Air Force One at Grand Canyon National Park Airport in Tusayan, Ariz., in 2009. (Dana Felthauser/Associated Press)

exhausted. He consumed her like oxygen. And the photograph became a social media phenomenon.

Arms: Michelle Obama's sculpted arms symbolized her strength and focus. They are post-Title IX arms — signaling a shift in the broader definition of femininity. She went sleeveless in the Capitol, at state dinners and the inaugural balls. Her arms were a point of admiration, controversy and irritation. New York Times columnist David Brooks referred to them as "thunder and lighting" and suggested they had been overexposed. They were a style asset, but they were also an entry point for a conversation about her body. And for all of those who coveted her muscular limbs, there were those whose consideration of them was the opening jab in a full-body assault.

FLOTUS's shorts: When the family vacationed at the Grand Canyon in 2009, Michelle Obama stepped off Air Force One wearing sneakers, a T-shirt, a pair of hiking shorts and an unbuttoned checked shirt that blew open as she walked. It was her Every Woman look, an awkward announcement that she intended to maintain a common touch.

POTUS's jeans: The president's jeans were out-of-date and awful. Baggy and faded. They were too short and sat too high on his waist. The candidate that hipster magazines had declared cool threw out the first pitch at the 2009 MLB All-Star Game wearing a pair of old dad jeans. In his own defense, Obama said he hates to shop. But he took note of the criticism. His swagger, after all, was part of his political capital. He modernized his denim.

POTUS's gait: He does not walk. He strolls with a black man's head-up posture. His gait is nonchalant but confident. His arms swing casually at his side; his posture is erect but not stiff. His walk is distinctive because it combines the personal grace of a jazz riff

President Obama waves as he jogs off the field after throwing out the first pitch at the MLB All-Star Game in St. Louis in July 2009. (Haraz N. Ghanbari/Associated Press)

Michelle Obama dances with students in Chicago in February 2013 to promote physical activity programs for children. (Tasos Katopodis/Getty Images)

Michelle Obama, right, along with daughters Sasha and Malia and mother Marian Robinson, attends President Obama's inauguration in 2009. (John McDonnell/The Washington Post)

Marian Robinson, the first lady's mother, takes a bow after dancing with children in Johannesburg in June 2011. Michelle Obama, Malia and Sasha Obama, and family members Avery Robinson and Leslie Robinson joined her. (Charles Dharapak/Agence France-Presse via Getty Images)

with the quiet awareness that people are always watching, sizing him up. Judging.

FLOTUS's gait: Michelle Obama doesn't slouch, but she walks with a heavy foot. There is nothing light about her stride. It is unrushed and sure. It suggests that she is grounded but also that she carries a weight.

FLOTUS's joie de vivre: So many times during her tenure in the East Wing, Michelle Obama rejected the formality and sobriety of the bully pulpit to sell her agenda of healthy eating, fitness and education. Instead, she danced with Ellen DeGeneres; she hula-hooped with kids; she rapped with Jay Pharoah; she sang karaoke with James Corden; she raced Jimmy Fallon through the White House in a potato sack. The byproduct of her joie de vivre campaign was to craft an image of a White House that was full of vigor and connected to popular culture. Meet folks where they are; that was her mantra.

Malia and Sasha: The Obama daughters rarely spoke in public. In the early days of their father's administration, in 2009, they read "Snowmen at Night" to young patients at Children's National Medical Center and the media listened in. Over the ensuing years they might have been overheard chatting with their parents or with each other. Mostly, though, they were seen and not heard. And when they were seen, their appearance was coordinated, edited, spit-shined and polished. From the jelly-bean-colored Crewcuts coats at the 2009 swearing-in to their grown-up Naeem Khan evening gowns at the state dinner in honor of Canada, the country watched the girls grow up. The passage of time was not marked by tales of middle school angst, teenage peer pressure or adolescent rebellion, but by the shift from princess coats and grosgrain ribbons to heels, cropped tops and makeup.

Vogue cover: Michelle Obama has appeared on the cover of Vogue three times. The first photograph had the weight of history. She was the breakthrough: an African American first lady. Her appearance on the fashion bible in 2009 was also a message to little girls and young women of color: You, too, are beautiful. The second cover in 2013 was more formal. Instead of depicting Obama as relatable mom in chief, it showed her in a more commanding posture — sitting upright, her arms at her sides. The third cover, in 2016, showed her with the tousled-hair glamour and cultural influence of a celebrity, someone not bound by the traditions and expectations of a first lady. It was an exit portrait.

Marian Robinson: Make no mistake, Marian Robinson is *not* the nation's grandmother. She is not ensconced on the third floor of the White House to reassure the country in times of trouble, to share homey recipes and advice with working mothers or to be a spokesperson for a fulfilling retirement. She is there for her family — because before they were the first family, global emblems of progress or targets for criticism, they were kin. She is not a symbol of normalcy, but she is a reminder that those sealed in the White House bubble need it, and she can provide a little of it. Photographers captured her traveling in South Africa with her daughter, with her family during the lighting of the National Christmas Tree. She had an unobstructed view of history without having to bear the weight of it. And no matter how much she might have wanted, she could not shoulder the burden — if only for a moment — just to give her loved ones a rest.

Michelle Obama on White House parenting: 'What on Earth am I doing to these babies?'

By Krissah Thompson and Neely Tucker

On the day that Michelle Obama sent her daughters off to a new elementary school in a big black SUV with gun-toting Secret Service agents, she said she thought to herself: "What on Earth am I doing to these babies?"

Her husband was among the youngest men to serve as president, and their attractive, youthful family drew the world's attention. Protecting their daughters from public scrutiny was a priority from the day he was elected.

The first lady committed herself to working no more than three days each week, calling herself "mom in chief," and let her staff know that Malia and Sasha's school events should be the first items added to her calendar.

President Obama, who had written in depth about his insecurities as a husband and father before his election, has said his wife encouraged him to be more involved in his daughters' lives. Over eight years, they painted a quotidian public portrait of their family life: dinner together whenever he was home; attendance at parent-teacher conferences; coaching the girls in basketball; mom and dad date night; and the girls' grandmother living with them to keep an eye out.

No family's inner workings are perfect. The president's aides often cited the time-consuming work of raising children as one reason Obama did not spend more time on the schmoozing and other niceties that political Washington expected of a president.

Barack Obama, then a senator and candidate for president, meets up with his family at a campaign stop in Pueblo, Colo., in 2008. (Linda Davidson/The Washington Post)

Yet, in a 2013 interview with CBS News, Michelle Obama referred to herself as a "busy single mother." It was a slip of the tongue that may have been Freudian, and she quickly tried to explain:

"When you've got a husband who is president, it can feel a little single," she joked. "But he's there."

Moments of candor around the travails of parenting — and the joy of it — have been a trademark of the Obamas' time in public life. Here is how they approached parenting — in their own words.

Barack Obama on the birth of his first child:

"For three magical months the two of us fussed and fretted over our new baby, checking the crib to make sure she was breathing, coaxing smiles from her, singing her songs, and taking so many pictures that we started to wonder if we were damaging her eyes. Suddenly our different biorhythms came in handy: While Michelle got some well-earned sleep, I would stay up until one or two in the morning, changing diapers, heating breast milk, feeling my daughter's soft breath against my chest as I rocked her to sleep, guessing at her infant dreams."

— "The Audacity of Hope," 2006

Michelle Obama on being a working mother:
"I took my last job [before my husband entered the White House] because of my boss's reaction to my family situation. I didn't have a babysitter, so I took Sasha right in there with me in her crib and her rocker. I was still nursing, so I was wearing my nursing shirt. I told my boss, "This is what I have: two small kids. My husband is running for the U.S. Senate. I will not work part time. I need flexibility. I need a good salary. I need to be able to afford babysitting. And if you can do all that, and you're willing to be flexible with me because I will get the job done, I can work hard on a flexible schedule." I was very clear. And he said yes to everything."
— White House Working Families Summit, June 2014

Michelle Obama on protecting her daughters:
"Malia and Sasha were little itty-bitties when we came into office. I mean, it still moves me to tears to think about the first day I put them in the car with their Secret Service agents to go to their first day of school. And I saw them leaving and I thought, what on Earth am I doing to these babies? So I knew right then and there my first job was to make sure they were going to be whole and normal and cared for in the midst of all this craziness."
— White House United State of Women Summit, June 2016

Michelle Obama on chores in the White House:
"The first thing I said to some of the staff when I did my visit because, of course, they're like, "Oh, the girls, they're so great." I said, you know, we're going to have to set up some boundaries because they're going to need to be able to make their beds and clean up."
— ABC News, November 2008

Barack Obama on arguing with his wife about balancing work and family:
"It's hard to argue with Michelle when she insists that the burdens of the modern family fall more heavily on the woman."
— Audacity of Hope, 2006

Ty Inc., the maker of Beanie Babies, debuted the dolls Sweet Sasha, left, and Marvelous Malia in January 2009. (Scott Olson/Getty Images)

Michelle Obama's press secretary in 2009 after Ty Inc., produced Beanie Babies dolls called Sweet Sasha and Marvelous Malia:

"We feel it is inappropriate to use young, private citizens for marketing purposes."

— Katie McCormick Lelyveld

The company quickly retired the dolls.

Barack Obama on his daughter's reaction to the Gulf of Mexico oil spill crisis:

"The Gulf is going to be affected in a bad way. And so my job right now is just to make sure that everybody in the Gulf understands this is what I wake up to in the morning and this is what I go to bed at night thinking about.

And it's not just me, by the way. When I woke this morning and I'm shaving and Malia knocks on my bathroom door and she peeks in her head and she says, "Did you plug the hole yet, Daddy?" Because I think everybody understands that when we are fouling the Earth like this, it has concrete implications not just for this generation, but for future generations."

— White House press conference, May 2010

Michelle Obama on raising teenagers with the president:
"The one thing he cares about is just look like you're listening to me."
— Jimmy Kimmel Live, October 2012

On requiring their daughters to work minimum wage jobs:
"I think every kid needs to get a taste of what it's like to do ... real hard work."
— Michelle Obama

"We are looking for opportunities for them to feel as if going to work and getting a paycheck is not always fun, not always stimulating, not always fair. But that's what most folks go through every single day."
— Barack Obama, Parade magazine, June 2014

Barack Obama on the passage of time while parenting:
"When I was first elected to this office, Malia was 10 and Sasha was just 7. And they grow up too fast. This fall, Malia heads off to college. And I'm starting to choke up."
— Canadian State Dinner, March 2016

The Obamas reflect on raising their daughters:
"If I think to myself, what's the thing that I'm going to remember on my last breath, it's not going to be anything to do with my office. I'm not going to be thinking about Grant Park and me getting elected. I'm not going to be thinking about even passing health care, as important as that has been. What I'm going to remember is me holding my daughter's hand, and walking her to the park, and seeing the sun go down, and pushing her on a swing."
— Barack Obama's question and answer session
with White House interns, December 2015

"I wake up every morning in a house that was built by slaves — and I watch my daughters — two beautiful, intelligent, black young women — playing with their dogs on the White House lawn."
— Michelle Obama's speech at the Democratic
National Convention, July 2016

The Obama-Biden bond is among the strongest in White House history

By Paul Kane

When Barack Obama arrived in Washington in 2005, the freshman senator from Illinois took his place in the very last seat on the far end of the dais of the Foreign Relations Committee. He was the most junior Democrat on a panel on which Joe Biden had served as chairman or ranking Democrat for more than a decade. The men were a generation apart, at least.

Biden, who entered the Senate when Obama was in junior high school, saw in Obama a fast learner but still viewed him mostly as an understudy.

The roles reversed when the upstart Obama captured the prize that Biden has coveted much of his professional life and invited the elder statesman to be a partner in his presidency.

By the end of their two terms in the White House, President Obama and Vice President Biden had forged a professional relationship and a personal bond that is deeper and stronger than any president and vice president in the modern era. They have agreed on almost every major policy issue in their eight years together, and when there has been disagreement, they managed to keep their disputes quietly behind the scenes.

Biden, notorious for speaking too much and revealing too much, has made his share of mistakes in that regard, but most were in the Washington tradition of telling the truth at the inappropriate time — such as his 2012 embrace of gay marriage before Obama made his own similar announcement. The vice president

President Obama and Vice President Biden ride in the motorcade on the way to the signing of the Dodd-Frank Wall Street Reform and Consumer Protection Act. (Pete Souza/The White House)

chafed at the way some of Obama's senior advisers threw their support behind Hillary Clinton's 2016 presidential campaign long before Biden made his own decision, and someone even leaked that during the 2012 reelection campaign, advisers polled whether replacing Biden with Clinton would give Obama a boost.

But the president never considered abandoning Biden, and throughout the 2016 primary campaign, he stayed publicly neutral. When it came time in October 2015 for Biden to announce that his days of running for office were done, Obama stood at his side in the Rose Garden. The president knew he was supporting a friend who was giving up on a lifelong dream of winning the presidency.

The distance they have traveled together can perhaps be best illustrated by two moments, eight years apart.

In February 2007, Biden announced his bid for the 2008 presidential nomination in a race that already included Clinton and Obama, prompting Biden to praise Obama as a rising star but in a manner that made clear he considered himself the wiser elder statesman. Biden fumbled his way through that backhanded compliment and walked into a racial quagmire.

"You got the first mainstream African American who is articulate and bright and clean and a nice-looking guy," Biden said at the time. "I mean, that's a storybook, man."

In early 2015, during one of their weekly lunch meetings, Biden explained the financial pressures his son's battle with brain cancer had created. He told Obama he was considering selling the family home outside Wilmington, Del., where he'd raised his children, to financially care for Beau Biden's family.

"Don't sell that house. Promise me you won't sell the house," Obama told Biden, according to the vice president's account in a CNN interview. "I'll give you the money. Whatever you need, I'll give you the money. Don't, Joe."

Biden did not need the loan, but a few months later his son lost his fight with cancer. Biden asked Obama to deliver Beau Biden's eulogy.

"To Joe and Jill: Just like everybody else here, Michelle and I thank God you are in our lives. Taking this ride with you is one of the great pleasures of our lives. Joe, you are my brother," Obama said, looking down directly at the vice president and his wife, Jill Biden.

Their backgrounds and personalities couldn't be more different. Obama is cerebral and disdains drama, while Biden is all heart and emotion and prone to theatrics in his own decision-making.

It is not the usual course of events for a president and vice president to remain close by the end of their service together. By 2008, Dick Cheney had grown resentful at how often he had been outflanked by other advisers to President George W. Bush. In 2000, Al Gore ran a presidential campaign that refused to use Bill Clinton because of Clinton's personal scandals.

Before them, Dan Quayle was never considered part of the innermost circle in George H.W. Bush's administration, and Bush himself felt like an outsider while serving as Ronald Reagan's vice president in the 1980s.

But Obama and Biden are viewed as so close that, in their last weeks in office, they even became a viral social media sensation after Republican Donald Trump's stunning victory over the presidential race. People posted pictures of the two men together, sometimes

President Obama and first lady Michelle Obama embrace Vice President Biden and Jill Biden moments after the television networks called the 2012 election in their favor. (Pete Souza/The White House)

hugging, sometimes holding hands, with parodied captions, all with the theme of Biden wanting to play tricks on Trump — such as stealing all the T's on West Wing keyboards. In the memes, Obama serves as the mature foil to his prankster friend.

The two families have also connected in a way that might lead them into the same social circles after they leave the White House. Obama's two daughters have attended Sidwell Friends School in Northwest Washington, where three of Biden's grandchildren have gone to school. Sasha Obama, the president's younger daughter, is in the same class as Maisy Biden, and the two are friendly enough that the vice president took them along on the delegation that attended the women's World Cup soccer championship in Canada in 2015.

Biden has lost plenty of his own internal West Wing policy battles, but he has declared that he will not write a tell-all book about those years together and instead might pen a more personal account of his family's journey.

Obama has made clear that his affection for his older partner will likely continue well past their time in the White House.

"I'm grateful every day that you've got such a big heart, and a big soul, and those broad shoulders," Obama told the vice president at Beau Biden's funeral. "I couldn't admire you more."

Seeking a presidential 'pawtograph': Letters from America's kids to the first dogs, Sunny and Bo

By Neely Tucker

It has to be said that Barack Obama was not really a dog kind of guy.

Didn't grow up with one. Wasn't a bachelor with a big, happy mutt. He and Michelle, as a new couple, didn't dote on a puppy before having kids.

He did not, in fact, get a dog until becoming president and arriving at 1600 Pennsylvania Ave., and only then to fulfill a campaign promise to his daughters. Malia was allergic to most dogs, but she and Sasha wanted a puppy.

"So whether we're going to be able to balance those two things, I think, is a pressing issue on the Obama household," he said in an interview while still president-elect.

See? The kids, talking him into it.

They were good lobbyists, though, and in April, three months after Obama took office, Bo, a black-and-white Portuguese water dog, moved in (the breed is hypoallergenic). The family had looked for a shelter dog, but Bo had been returned to a breeder in Texas, which made it a good compromise. Sen. Ted Kennedy (a dog guy), who had obtained one of his dogs from the same breeder, made Bo a gift to the Obamas.

Sunny, a female of the same breed, arrived four years later.

The president seemed to enjoy the dogs during his two terms, but you had the sense that this was in the role of Being a Good

ABOVE: President Obama, first lady Michelle Obama and daughters Malia and Sasha officially introduce Bo, their Portuguese water dog, on the White House South Lawn in 2009. (Bill O'Leary/The Washington Post) BELOW: Michelle Obama follows daughters Malia, center, and Sasha as they arrive to welcome the official White House Christmas tree on Nov. 28, 2014. Malia has Bo on a leash, and Sasha is walking Sunny. (Susan Walsh/Associated Press)

Dad. The outdoor pictures of him with the dogs are mostly with the whole family out walking. He's usually wearing a tie, if not a suit.

"Some of my fondest memories of the White House are just being with the girls on a summer night and walking the dogs around the South Lawn, talking and listening to them, trying to get Bo to move because sometimes it's hot," he told Essence magazine in an end-of-term interview.

Lyndon B. Johnson, when he picked up his beagle by the ears and people got upset? Bill Clinton with Buddy the chocolate Lab? George W. Bush with Barney the Scottish terrier, scampering around the White House with the Barney-cam?

You got the idea those were dog guys, with or without kids.

Richard Nixon, dragging his dog Checkers into an allegation of campaign finance irregularities?

You just felt bad for the dog.

Still, it's fair to say the first dogs of the Obama administration were rock stars. Their schedule was so packed that they had a monthly agenda of appearances, overseen and approved by the first lady. They were regulars at the White House Easter Egg Roll and on Christmas visits to hospitals. They sometimes visited with foreign dignitaries at the White House, and the first lady was accompanied by Bo on White House tours she gave on her husband's inaugural anniversary.

Children wrote them fan letters, because it is an American thing to do.

Dear Bo and Sunny Obama, My Name is [REDACTED] and I am a third grade student at [REDACTED]. I am 8 years old. I live with my mom, dad, an older brother named [REDACTED] and my uncle. I am Etopian. My favorite subject is math. And my favorite subject to study is history. Do you have a place to play in or out of the White House? And do you like to play a lot? I think you should behave yourselves in the White House. Can you ask the president if he enjoys walking you at least 50%? P.S. Can you send a picture tvo me? A Good Citizen, [REDACTED]

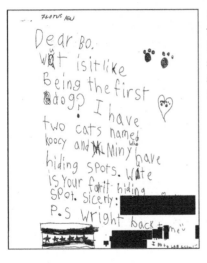

Dear Bo, I love dogs. Do you like the White House? What is your favorite food? Can I your pawtograph please? I think you're cute. Your friend, [REDACTED]

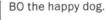

Dear Bo, Wut is it like being the first dog? I have two cats names Koocy and Miny who have hiding spots. What is your favrit hiding spot. Sicerly: [REDACTED]
P.S. Wright back to me :)

BO the happy dog.

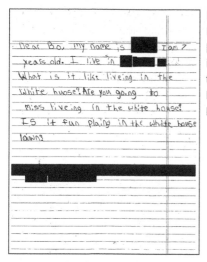

Dear Bo, My name is [REDACTED]. I am 7 years old. I live in [REDACTED]. What is it like living in the white huose? Are you going to miss liveing in the white house? Is it fun playing in the white house lawn?

Dear Bo and Sunny, My Great-Grandma is helping me to write. My name is [REDACTED] and I love my dog. My dog is smart just like you. Did you have to go to puppy school? We would like to hear from you. Please could I have a picture too? Thank you, [REDACTED]

"They can sit on my lap, they sit on my chair, they cuddle with me," Michelle Obama said in early 2016.

No word from the president about whether they could sit on his lap, or on his chair. But like most presidents, as Harry S. Truman observed, it's not likely that he had any doubts about who two of his most loyal friends were in this town.

CREDITS

EDITING

Terence Samuel, project editor
Allison Michaels, project manager, digital editor
Shannon Croom, multiplatform editor
Courtney Rukan, multiplatform editor
Emily Chow, graphics assignment editor
Seth Blanchard, digital project design
Emily Yount, digital project design

ILLUSTRATIONS

Suzette Moyer, art director
James Steinberg, illustrator (The First Black President)
Brian Stauffer, illustrator (Commander in Chief)
Thandiwe Tshabalala, illustrator (Obama's America)
Jasu Hu, illustrator (Obama and the World)
Erin K. Robinson, illustrator (The First Family)

PHOTO EDITING

Stephen Cook
Robert Miller
Kenneth Dickerman

Wendy Galietta
Bronwen Latimer
Dee Swann

WRITING AND REPORTING

Derek Chollet
Scott Clement
Elliot Cohen
Ivo H. Daalder
Mike DeBonis
Karen DeYoung
Juliet Eilperin
Thomas Gibbons-Neff
Robin Givhan
Emily Guskin
Will Haygood
Sari Horwitz
Greg Jaffe
Peniel Joseph

Paul Kane
Wesley Lowery
David Maraniss
Greg Miller
Steven Mufson
David Nakamura
John Pomfret
Missy Ryan
Peter Slevin
Kevin Sullivan
Krissah Thompson
Neely Tucker
William Wan

CPSIA information can be obtained
at www.ICGtesting.com
Printed in the USA
BVOW06s0028300117

474726BV00002B/2/P